Developing in Two Languages

Child Language and Child Development: Multilingual–Multicultural Perspectives

Series Editor: Professor Li Wei, *University of Newcastle-upon-Tyne, UK*

Editorial Advisors:
Professor Gina Conti-Ramsden, *University of Manchester, UK*
Professor Kevin Durkin, *The University of Western Australia*
Professor Susan Ervin-Tripp, *University of California, Berkeley, USA*
Professor Jean Berko Gleason, *Boston University, USA*
Professor Brian MacWhinney, *Carnegie Mellon University, USA*

Children are brought up in diverse yet specific cultural environments; they are engaged from birth in socially meaningful and appropriate activities; their development is affected by an array of social forces. This book series is a response to the need for a comprehensive and interdisciplinary documentation of up-to-date research on child language and child development from a multilingual and multicultural perspective. Publications from the series will cover language development of bilingual and multilingual children, acquisition of languages other than English, cultural variations in child rearing practices, cognitive development of children in multicultural environments, speech and language disorders in bilingual children and children speaking languages other than English, and education and healthcare for children speaking non-standard or non-native varieties of English. The series will be of particular interests to linguists, psychologists, speech and language therapists, and teachers, as well as to other practitioners and professionals working with children of multilingual and multicultural backgrounds.

Recent Books in the Series
Culture-Specific Language Styles: The Development of Oral Narrative and Literacy
    Masahiko Minami
Language and Literacy in Bilingual Children
    D. Kimbrough Oller and Rebecca E. Eilers (eds)
Phonological Development in Specific Contexts: Studies of Chinese-Speaking Children
    Zhu Hua
Bilingual Children's Language and Literacy Development
    Roger Barnard and Ted Glynn (eds)

Other Books of Interest
Foundations of Bilingual Education and Bilingualism
    Colin Baker
Encyclopedia of Bilingualism and Bilingual Education
    Colin Baker and Sylvia Prys Jones
Multicultural Children in the Early Years
    P. Woods, M. Boyle and N. Hubbard
Working with Bilingual Children
    M.K. Verma, K.P. Corrigan and S. Firth (eds)
Young Bilingual Children in Nursery School
    Linda Thompson

For more details of these or any other of our publications, please contact:
Multilingual Matters, Frankfurt Lodge, Clevedon Hall,
Victoria Road, Clevedon, BS21 7HH, England
http://www.multilingual-matters.com

CHILD LANGUAGE AND CHILD DEVELOPMENT 5
Series Editor: Li Wei, University of Newcastle

Developing in Two Languages
Korean Children in America

Sarah J. Shin

MULTILINGUAL MATTERS LTD
Clevedon • Buffalo • Toronto

Library of Congress Cataloging in Publication Data
Shin, Sarah J.
Developing in Two Languages: Korean Children in America/Sarah J. Shin.
Child Language and Child Development: 5
Includes bibliographical references and index.
1. Bilingualism in children–United States. 2. Korean American children–Language.
I. Title. II. Series.
P115.2.S5 2004
404'.2'08309073–dc22   2004002920

British Library Cataloguing in Publication Data
A catalogue entry for this book is available from the British Library.

ISBN 1-85359-747-3 (hbk)
ISBN 1-85359-746-5 (pbk)

Multilingual Matters Ltd
UK: Frankfurt Lodge, Clevedon Hall, Victoria Road, Clevedon BS21 7HH.
USA: UTP, 2250 Military Road, Tonawanda, NY 14150, USA.
Canada: UTP, 5201 Dufferin Street, North York, Ontario M3H 5T8, Canada.

Typeset by Patrick Armstrong Book Production Services.
Printed and bound in Great Britain by the Cromwell Press Ltd.

Contents

Acknowledgments

I would like to express my deepest gratitude to the following individuals who have provided me with insightful and critical comments on earlier drafts of this book: Donna Christian, Jodi Crandall, Susan Gelman, Rosina Lippi-Green, Lesley Milroy, Barbara Zurer Pearson, Robert Rubinstein, Sung Yon Ryoo, Joe Stone, John M. Swales, G. Richard Tucker, and Guadalupe Valdés. Responsibility for any shortcomings is entirely my own. I am especially thankful to Li Wei for encouraging me to publish this book in the Child Language and Child Development series, and to Wendy Saul and Kendra Wallace for inspiring me to write not only with my brain but also with my heart. Young-chan Han and Linda Won of Howard County Public Schools (Maryland) have provided me with stimulating discussions on Korean American families and commented on various portions of the manuscript. It is heartening to know that such dedicated individuals are working tirelessly to advocate for language minority students and families.

I am grateful to various publishers for permission to reprint adapted versions of papers published in their journals. Chapter 5 is an adapted version of my paper with Lesley Milroy, 'Bilingual language acquisition by Korean schoolchildren in New York City', in *Bilingualism: Language and Cognition* (Cambridge University Press), and part of Chapter 4 has been adapted from my paper (also with Lesley Milroy) in the *International Journal of Bilingualism* (Kingston Press Services Ltd), titled 'Conversational codeswitching among Korean–English bilingual children'. Part of Chapter 6 which deals with birth order differences in bilingual experiences has been adapted from my paper, 'Birth order and the language experience of bilingual children', published in the *TESOL Quarterly* (TESOL).

Needless to say, this study could not have been made possible without the help of my twelve Korean informants and their parents, as well as the many Korean American families who have participated in the survey and interviews. My sincere heartfelt thanks go to them. Over the years, I have had the distinct privilege of getting to know many wonderful parents, grandparents and children who have entrusted me with their stories of adapting to life in America. My interactions with them have no doubt significantly influenced the way I think about the education of language minority children. I am indebted to Ellie Chung Glus for her excellent support and encouragement throughout my fieldwork in New York City.

She played a central role in helping me obtain access to my informants and made the huge task of data collection seem much less daunting. Lastly, I would like to thank my husband, Yoon Ki Shin, for his extraordinary encouragement and patience, and my sons, Isaac and Joshua, whose developing bilingualism continually fascinates me and to whom this book is dedicated.

Introduction

As an English as a second language (ESL) teacher educator, I am frequently asked whether or not teachers should allow language minority students to speak their native languages in the classroom. When I ask my teacher candidates this question, the answer that I get most often is that only beginning ESL students should be allowed to use their first languages and that as students gain more proficiency in English, they should gradually decrease their use of the native language. Teachers argue that ESL students come to school to learn English and time spent speaking the first language is time that could have been spent learning English. Some go so far as to say that the only way to really learn a second language well is through total immersion and, therefore, students should not be allowed to speak their native languages at all. Others take a more democratic approach by saying that allowing native language use in the classroom is unfair for students who do not have classmates that share the same first language. I then ask the teachers, 'If you were an immigrant student in a foreign country and your teacher tells you that you can't use English in school, how would you feel?'. Some then say that they would feel badly about their language and may even be ashamed of their background.

Many well-meaning teachers insist that their linguistic minority students speak only English in the classroom because they think that students' native languages may interfere with their acquisition of English. For others, the presence of another language in the classroom is simply a distraction – teachers may feel uncomfortable not knowing whether students who speak other languages are properly engaged in classroom tasks. Whatever the reasoning may be however, a great deal of research shows that quite contrary to popular assumption that native language hinders second language acquisition, the use of the first language in instructional contexts helps students develop a conceptual and linguistic proficiency that is strongly related to the development of literacy in the second language (see, for example, Cummins, 1996; Lanauze & Snow, 1989). Moreover, strong support of immigrant children's first languages throughout schooling contributes significantly to academic success (August & Hakuta, 1997; Collier, 1992; Freeman & Freeman, 2000; Ramirez, 1992). Students who are allowed to develop their native languages to high

1

levels of proficiency while learning English have clear academic advantages over students whose first languages are not supported (Shannon, 1999; Snow, 1990). Much of the research that highlights the benefits of first language development in linguistic minority children shows that proficiency in another language is an advantage, not an obstacle to growth and achievement.

In this book, my arguments are also based on the assumption that sustained native-language development in immigrant children is beneficial for the individual, family and society. I have no doubt that my own background as a so-called 1.5-generation Korean American has influenced my interest and theoretical inclination in this research. Having immigrated to the United States at the age of 13, I grew up wanting to be a monolingual English speaker. As strange as this may sound to some people, I often pretended that I did not know my native language. I remember coming home feeling absolutely miserable on my first day of school in the United States and telling my parents that I wanted to go back to Korea. I had been placed in a remedial math class where the teacher struggled to teach fractions to a group of highly unruly and disruptive students. Having studied fractions at least several years before, I knew that the school considered me stupid simply because I did not speak English. As the semester progressed, I saw that those who got along well in school, many of whom were of language minority backgrounds, spoke only English. I concluded that as far as school was concerned, my ability to speak, read and write Korean did not have any value. In fact, my proficiency in Korean was a sign to everyone that I was a new immigrant – poor, unsophisticated and marginal. I wanted people to think that I could speak perfect English with no trace of a foreign accent and that although I look Asian, I was born in America and grew up speaking only English. It was not until much later that I realized that my native language and culture were a treasure, not a problem.

This book is, first and foremost, an account of the language situation of Korean immigrant children and their families. Today, Koreans are a visible and significant part of American schools and society, with over one million Korean Americans living across the United States (ranked fifth in number among the Asian and Pacific Islander populations according to the 2000 US Census). However, there are currently no book-length descriptions of the language situation of bilingual Korean–English children. This book is an attempt to address this gap by providing a culturally and sociolinguistically sensible picture of the language development of Korean American children. In addition, this book has a broader, more general goal of portraying children's bilingualism as a dynamic entity, whose development is continuously shaped by a multitude of linguistic, social, cultural and educational factors. I shall argue that the bilingualism of linguistic minority children is a resource to be cultivated and not a problem to be overcome.

'Model Minority'?

Korean Americans, like some of the other Asian ethnic groups, are often viewed as a 'model minority'. The popular perception of Asian Americans is that they have done remarkably well in achieving 'the American dream' of getting a good education and working hard to make a good living. As a result of changes in US immigration law in 1965, the influx of highly educated immigrants from Korea, Hong Kong, Taiwan, India and the Philippines bolstered the positive image of Asian Americans as an intelligent, industrious and highly successful model minority that have overcome barriers facing recent immigrants (Hurh, 1998: 95). Children of these Asian immigrant groups (including Koreans) have indeed tended to excel in scholastic achievement, compared to other minority groups in America. However, the 'model minority' stereotype and the social and economic success of some Asian immigrants mask a deeper underlying problem of isolation, cultural discontinuity and identity conflict that many Korean (and other Asian) children experience while navigating the worlds of the home and the school. Living in the intersection of two cultures with different modes of discourses and expectations, they are pushed and pulled by various forces of assimilation, traditional values and family pressures, which often leave them confused and lost. In this book, I am chiefly interested in the role that language plays in the lives of these children and how their bilingualism is influenced by the various conflicting forces.

In many cases, the deeper underlying problems of linguistic, cultural and identity conflict are worsened because many Korean parents and children cannot communicate with one another due to a lack of a common language. Second-generation Korean Americans often voice their frustration that their parents have not tried hard enough to learn English. The parents, in contrast, feel that their children are challenging their authority as parents. It is not unusual for 10 or 11 year olds to help their limited English-proficient parents to open a bank account or even buy a car. While this sort of language brokering offers the parents the badly needed help they require to live in America, it also sometimes results in children taking on authority and losing respect for their parents.[1] In fact, there is often a 'tug of war' between immigrant parents and their children, as news-reporter, Claudio Sanchez, described at the Second Heritage Languages in America Conference (2002). Sanchez explained that while parents are driven by a survival instinct that drives them to work their bodies to the limit to make ends meet, their children desperately try to fit into the mainstream society, which sees immigrants as trivial and undesirable.

Immigrant parents and children often have very different life experiences and share little in common in terms of language, values and dispositions. In many cases, the parents work long hours to provide for their families and have little time or energy left to spend with their children or to learn English. In a survey of Korean junior and senior high school students in New York City, 64% of the sample reported that neither of their parents was at home after school and 46% indicated that no one at all was home after school (Min, 1995: 226). Due to their lack of English skills, first–generation immigrants are forced to take low-paying jobs that do not require the use of much English. Immigrants often associate with fellow countrymen for psychological support and relief from the pressures of living in a foreign country. They listen to Korean music, watch TV programs in Korean and read Korean newspapers to be informed of world and local events. The children, in contrast, are educated in English, associate with English speakers and are Americanized in their thinking. They listen to popular music in English, watch American shows on TV and navigate the very different worlds of the home with traditional ethnic values and customs, and the school, which promotes English monolingualism and assimilation. When children go to school, they try very hard to fit into the majority group by talking and acting like whites and some may even fantasize themselves as being white for some time. Children become increasingly American in their thinking and view of the world and, in their attempt to identify with the majority population, may lose even the little Korean they used to know before entering school.

As children speak English at home, parents also switch over to it, at least in speaking with the children. Parents often learn enough English to carry on simple conversations with their children and their English abilities may improve over time, albeit slowly. Some parents reason that their own skills in English may improve from speaking English with their children and that speaking English at home might help the children in school. Indeed, many immigrant parents are advised by teachers and doctors to stop speaking the native language and to speak English at home so that children can adapt more easily to the language of the school. Furthermore, the idea that acquiring one language must be easier than learning two makes intuitive sense to many parents who faithfully follow the advice of the professionals. However, parents often do not reach the level of proficiency in English that is required to sustain conversations requiring more sophisticated English skills. As children mature and become capable of more complex thoughts, parents find it increasingly difficult to communicate adequately with their children in their limited English. Meanwhile, due to lack of opportunities to practice the native language, the children have now lost even the little knowledge they had of their mother tongue and, therefore, cannot talk to their parents in that language. This is often when parents wonder whether their children would have learned English well anyway (even without the family shifting to English) and whether they should have maintained the use of the native language despite pressures to forego of it. Parents feel a deep sense of loss, as having heart-to-heart talks with their mostly English-speaking children proves to be impossible. Many issues are left untouched, countless feelings unexplored.

This, however, does not mean that there are no feelings to be shared. If parents cannot talk to their children, they cannot teach them what is right and what is wrong, nor can they pass down their values on why one should live as a responsible member of society. It is only obvious then how lack of parent–child communication (caused surely in part by a language barrier among other factors) can lead to societal problems as evidenced by some criminal cases involving Korean American teenagers. Goldberg (1995: 48) poignantly describes the utter devastation felt by parents whose children have become involved with Korean gangs:

> The parents stand there, waiting patiently for attention, the father red-faced, the mother crying into her hand. They've come to report a missing child, or to collect a son, or even a daughter, arrested for running with a gang. This is another way in which the dynamic of the melting pot has changed: Assimilation is no longer the exalting process once imagined by fifties and sixties liberals. For many morally upright immigrants, it now means watching sons and daughters turn into miscreants, petty criminals, or worse.

It is not my intention to discuss family problems of Korean Americans in this book. However, countless anecdotes and observations of Korean American families clearly indicate that a language barrier between parents and children is a major difficulty that has all sorts of ramifications for family and social dynamics as well as individual well-being. It is my intention to argue that although the social and personal pressures to abandon the minority language are indeed enormous, immigrants do not always have to make a choice between English and their mother tongue.

The Plight of Immigrant Parents

As a mother of American-born Korean children, I see how tremendously difficult it is to raise children bilingually in a mostly monolingual society. In an effort to help our children establish proficiency in Korean in an

English-speaking environment, my husband and I have been trying to speak and read mostly Korean at home to our children (Baker, 2000). Our American neighbors and Korean friends ask us, however, whether speaking mostly Korean will make it difficult for our children to transition into an all-English-speaking environment when they enter school. They wonder whether our boys will be able to learn English quickly enough. My concern, however, is not whether they will learn English well (they will, for sure) but that they might lose Korean. Despite what my husband and I have been trying to do to promote our children's acquisition of Korean at home, I worry that their future teachers might not value their heritage culture and language. I wonder if some of their teachers might forbid them from speaking Korean with other Korean children in the classroom. I worry that their teachers might convey to them directly or indirectly that speaking Korean is shameful and that 'real Americans speak English'. I know how great the pressure to speak English and to 'act American' can be for language-minority schoolchildren. I worry that, like many children of immigrants, my two boys might grow up wanting to dissociate themselves from their Korean roots.

When our older son turned three, my husband and I discussed long and hard the advantages and disadvantages of sending him to preschool. Since there are no bilingual or Korean language preschools in the area where we live, our choice was limited to English-speaking preschools. We knew the advantages of early childhood education and how our son could benefit from interacting with children his age in an intellectually stimulating environment. Yet, given the research evidence that the earlier the exposure to English is, the lower the proficiency in immigrant children's mother tongue (Hakuta and D'Andrea, 1992; Wong Fillmore, 1991), we also knew that preschool education in English posed a real threat to his Korean, which was still in its early stages of development. After much discussion, we decided to send him to a two-afternoons-a-week program for minimum exposure to English.

At the preschool, our son was fortunate to have a teacher who valued his language and cultural background and did not pressure him to produce native-like English utterances quickly. She allowed him to work at his own pace while giving him timely guidance in a supportive manner. During parent–teacher conferences, my son's teacher told me that he is quite a bright child even though he rarely speaks up in class. I really appreciated that she was able to recognize his cognitive abilities despite his lack of English. But I worry that some of his future teachers might not be as understanding as this teacher of the wealth of cultural knowledge and resources he brings from home. Sometimes I lie awake at night worrying about my children's educational journey in a country that is often hostile to minorities and immigrants. On the one hand, I would like my children to grow up bilingual, be able to participate in both cultures and be proud of their heritage as Korean and American. I know this would mean that there must be much concerted effort to promote their development and maintenance of Korean, the socially weaker language. On the other hand, I fear that our children might have teachers and classmates who may consider them inferior because they speak a minority language and have less than a perfect command of English. As a mother, I want to spare them the pain of being marginalized and provide them with all the necessary means to participate on an equal footing with mainstream children.

For this reason, a part of me wants to take the easy way out and speak only English to my children. Sometimes I even reason that my children's children and grandchildren will probably be monolingual English-speaking anyway and that whatever I do now to pass on Korean to my children is not likely to have any long-term effect. But as much as I would like to think that my children can blend in this society and be considered only based on their skills and not by their appearance, I also know the harsh realities of racism and prejudice, which permeate all educational and social establishments. As ethnic minorities, my sons will always be perceived as being different from the mainstream Anglo populations and even be held responsible for not knowing their ethnic language and culture. I often hear stories of Korean American college graduates who are turned down by companies that do business in Korea. They are devastated when they hear their interviewers say to them, 'If you're Korean, why can't you speak Korean?'. It is paradoxical that these individuals are suddenly held responsible for not knowing their native language, on which, all throughout their lives, they have been made to turn their backs. Herein lies the curse of being a language-minority – you are damned if you speak your mother tongue, and damned if you do not.

Over the years, I have seen many immigrant parents despair over their children's education. On the one hand, parents want their children to succeed in America, be well educated and make a good living. One of the perennial concerns of immigrant parents of young children is that their children will not learn English quickly enough and thus fall behind in school. For this reason, many parents try to expose their children to English early. Parents know all too well the heavy price of not knowing English well. On the other hand, with lack of English skills and knowledge about American school system, parents find it very difficult to appreciate how much English their children can really understand, what they have studied and how they are behaving in school (see also Valdés, 1996). When invited to attend parent–teacher conferences and other school-related events, parents are at first gripped with fear of not being able to communicate with their children's teachers, which is frustrating and humiliating. It is enormously stressful to manage long working hours, family responsibilities and children's education, all in a linguistically and culturally foreign environment. This leads to 'a sense of powerlessness among Korean parents in their homes, as they watch America turn their children into people they don't fully understand – that is, Americans' (Goldberg, 1995: 46).

Many immigrant parents struggle with an extreme lack of resources to support native-language development in children. For example, good heritage-language schools are in considerably short supply in many immigrant communities. Even if minority language schools do exist, they are often of such low quality that parents end up sending their children to higher quality mainstream schools with better curriculum and teachers. There is also difficulty in finding children's books in the native language and providing children with opportunities to speak it with peers in meaningful contexts. The home is often the last stronghold against the overwhelming influence of English. Without successful intergenerational transmission of the mother tongue, no amount of maintenance efforts can keep the minority language from disappearing (Fishman, 1991). However, English creeps into even the most linguistically fortified families where there is a household ban on English. The fight to keep the minority language alive is an uphill battle and parents often lack the necessary means to protect the home against the steady advances of English.

In this book, I will show ways in which various educational, social and economic pressures push parents to forego educating their children in the mother tongue. Immigrant parents are well aware of the practical value of knowing English for a comfortable and respectable life in America. Since lack of English skills is what prevented them from properly participating in mainstream society, immigrant parents are determined to see their children become fully competent in English. In addition to personal and economic motivations however, many language decisions made by immigrant parents are based on popular myths around being bilingual. One such myth is that it is better for children to be exposed to one language and learn it well than to be exposed to two and learn neither one completely. Immigrant parents the world over are frequently advised by teachers, doctors and speech therapists to stop speaking the native language at home so as not to confuse children with input from two languages. However, rarely would American parents be told to stop speaking English at home so that their children can learn another language well at school. This book has the goal of shedding light on some of these myths of bilingualism and exploring the processes of bilingual development among Korean children growing up in America. This book will discuss some of the factors that contribute to some immigrant families to successfully raise their children as bilinguals and others to shift completely to English. It also discusses the role of schools and educational policies in discouraging the use of minority languages and makes recommendations for successfully developing and maintaining bilingual competence in linguistic minority children.

In writing this book, I think my experiences first as an ESL student, then later as a teacher educator and parent of ESL students have helped me to have linguistically and culturally nuanced perspectives on the many issues involved in the education of bilingual children. However, as Zentella (1997) points out, the closer the researcher is to the group, the more myopic the researcher may become about the significance of everyday acts that group members take for granted. I am well aware that the picture that I portray in this book on the bilingualism of Korean American children will never be a complete one as bilingualism itself is never a static entity. Nonetheless, I am charged to tell the story I know.

Data Sources

The data for this book come from four separate sources. The first source is the bilingual speech of 12 first-grade Korean American children in a New York City public school. Growing up as members of the Korean immigrant community in New York City, the children have all entered school with Korean as their mother tongue and they are acquiring English as a second language during childhood. The language data of the Korean American children were collected in May and June of 1995 in a mainstream first-grade classroom. I chose this class because I knew the teacher very well and because it contained 12 Korean students, an exceptional opportunity. Audio-recordings of the Korean children's natural spontaneous speech in various school situations were made over a two-month fieldwork period during which I carried out participant observation as a teacher's assistant. Detailed background information on the 12 Korean American children, the school and the teacher, as well as explanations of my role as a participant observer and audio-recording procedures can be found in Chapter 3.

The second source is the experimental language data elicited from the 12 Korean American children. This set of data investigates the extent to which the Korean American children have acquired the grammatical feature of plural-marking in Korean and in English. The plural marking feature was specifically selected for investigation because it presented the greatest problem for the Korean American children among about a dozen English grammatical morphemes. I shall compare the results of the bilingual children with those of same-age monolingual children of either language and discuss crosslinguistic influences in bilingual acquisition.

The third source is a survey of 251 Korean parents of school-age children in America. The survey contained 53 questions in Korean intended to elicit information about various aspects of bilingualism and language shift and maintenance in Korean American families. The parents were solicited through Korean American churches in Baltimore, Chicago, Houston and New York. This survey explores Korean American parents' language use and attitude toward bilingualism as well as family literacy practices in both languages.

Finally, follow-up interviews with selected survey respondents and their children were used. Interviews were conducted with 12 participants from the survey who were not related to the children studied in the New York City school. In addition, observations in Korean homes were conducted at various times over a period of four years. Family members were observed for their language choice and language-switching patterns. Notes were also made of home literacy patterns, including the availability of printed materials in both languages and literacy activities that occurred in those languages.

All these sources of data are described in detail in Chapter 3.

Organization of the Book

Chapter 1: The development of childhood bilingualism

The first chapter sets the stage for investigating bilingualism in language minority children. I discuss some of the common myths around being bilingual and present a sociolinguistically sound definition of bilingualism which looks at a bilingual as a fully competent speaker/hearer who uses his/her two languages for different purposes in different settings. Then I discuss codeswitching as a valuable communicative strategy available to bilingual speakers. I review the processes underlying simultaneous and successive acquisition of two languages during childhood and the role of the family and the school in socializing bilingual children. Then I look at different models of bilingual education and why some children develop and maintain functional bilingualism into adulthood while others become monolingual in the socially dominant language. I also discuss issues related to mother-tongue maintenance and loss by linguistic minority children.

Chapter 2: Koreans in the United States

Chapter 2 provides an overview of the economic and political circumstances of Korean immigration to the United States and characteristics of Korean communities in the USA. I present a brief history of Korean immigration to the United States beginning with labor immigration to Hawaii in the early 1900s and peaking in full-scale family immigration after the passage of the Immigration and Naturalization Act of 1965. I discuss education as an important motive for immigration and the soaring popularity of English in Korea today. I also review the social networks of Korean Americans and explain the role of the Korean Christian church in ethnic language and cultural maintenance by first- and second-generation Korean Americans.

Chapter 3: Methods

This chapter lays out the methodology used to obtain the data for this study. I first describe my access to the New York City public school, where I collected spontaneous and experimental bilingual speech data of 12 first-grade Korean American children. I describe the children, the teacher and the school and explain procedures for eliciting the children's spontaneous speech in the classroom. I then explain the experimental procedures used to determine the extent of the children's acquisition of grammatical morphemes in English and the plural feature in both languages. I also describe procedures for obtaining survey data on Korean American parents' language use, attitude and literacy patterns.

Chapter 4: Codeswitching as a communicative resource

Language mixing is veritably a crucial element of the bilingual speech of Korean American children. In this chapter, I present a detailed turn-by-turn, sequential analysis of the New York City Korean children's conversational codeswitching strategies and show ways in which the children skillfully negotiate the language for the interaction and accommodate other's language competences and preferences. In all, codeswitching is socially and pragmatically motivated and is not a result of the children's inability to keep the two languages apart. I show ways in which the children use codeswitching precisely and purposefully to convey their meanings and provide evidence that, far from being a distraction, mother-tongue use in the classroom is helpful for learning the second language as well as the subject matter.

Chapter 5: Dual language development

The Korean American children of this study learn to speak Korean at home and are later exposed to English in school. English is, therefore, acquired as a second language during childhood while Korean is still developing. Chapter 5 looks at aspects of the children's bilingual development. Specifically, I compare the extent of acquisition of English grammatical morphemes by the Korean children with that of children of other first-language backgrounds and explore ways in which the first language influences the course of development of second-language grammatical features. I also present results of an experimental study, which investigates plural marking in Korean and English. I show that the children, in most respects, follow similar but delayed patterns of first-language acquisition of Korean and second language acquisition of English. I also show evidence that suggests that the second-language influences the course of development of the first language in young bilingual children. I discuss the implications of these results in relation to what realistically constitutes a bilingual, as well as to educational policies concerning language minority children.

Chapter 6: Pressures for language shift

In this chapter, I explore the personal, social and educational pressures that contribute to language shift in the Korean American family and community. I present evidence that suggests that parental emphasis on education and desire to see children develop fluent and unaccented English contributes greatly to an overall shift to English in the Korean American family. I also discuss the serious consequences of poor advice given to parents by ill-informed teachers, doctors and speech therapists to stop speaking the native language to children at home so as not to confuse them with input from two languages. Furthermore, I examine ways in which English-only policies and the current national emphasis on educational testing drive parents to abandon the transmission and maintenance of their native language.

Chapter 7: Developing and maintaining heritage languages

This concluding chapter summarizes the major findings in the preceding chapters and offers suggestions for promoting the acquisition and maintenance of heritage languages by language minority children. It emphasizes the importance of educating parents of the facts and myths of bilingualism and provides practical recommendations for successful intergenerational transmission of the mother tongue. It also discusses ways in which minority languages can be integrated into regular school programs and how communities and institutions can support their maintenance.

Chapter 1

The Development of Childhood Bilingualism

Bilingualism is a fact of life for the majority of the world's population. Indeed it is estimated that about two-thirds of the world's population is bilingual (Baker & Prys Jones, 1998). There are anywhere between 5000 and 6000 languages in the world today (Grimes, 2000) and only about 190 countries in which to house them (World Almanac, 2003), which indicate how widespread language contact within individual countries must be. Although the ability to use two or more languages is, therefore, more common than monolingual competence (Mackey, 1967), bilingualism has traditionally been treated as a special case or a deviation from the monolingual norm (Romaine, 1995: 8). Most linguistic research has tended to focus on monolinguals and has treated bilinguals as exceptions. For instance, Chomsky's (1965: 3) theory of grammar is concerned primarily with 'an ideal speaker–listener, in a completely homogeneous speech-community, who knows its language perfectly.' Given the emphasis on describing the linguistic competence of the ideal monolingual speaker, bilingualism has necessarily been regarded as problematic, an impure form of communication by people who do not seem to know either language fully.

Strictly speaking, it would be difficult to find someone who thinks bilingualism is downright bad. After all, one can reasonably argue that knowing two languages is always better than knowing one. Indeed many people think that bilingualism (or multilingualism) is a sign of intellectual prowess and sophistication – those who have competence in several languages are often regarded with envy and admiration. However, unlike in many European and African countries where it is considered a valuable asset, bilingualism in the United States is often treated as a problem and a stigma. This is because those who are bilingual in the US are usually poor and from immigrant and/or racial minority backgrounds. The attitude of the Anglo-American majority and of the general public is that individuals of language minority backgrounds should be rapidly integrated into English-speaking mainstream society. The bilingualism of immigrant populations indicates that they are (still) speaking their minority languages, which is interpreted as resistance to a full integration into American society. As Grosjean (1982: 66) put it: 'The pressure to Americanize and to become monolingual in English has led the country into a bizarre paradox: most Americans, many of whose families are originally of a foreign language background, prove to be extremely incompetent in learning and speaking foreign languages.' Obviously not all bilingualism is alike. Indeed, while the bilingualism of majority English-speaking populations is prized and appreciated, the bilingualism of minority groups is considered a liability.

Compared to other language-related disciplines, bilingualism is a relatively new field of study and currently rather poorly understood. Systematic studies of childhood bilingualism, in particular, are severely lacking compared to studies of the development of monolingual children. We currently know relatively little about why and how some children become bilingual while others do not. Much more research would be required of different groups of children who take different routes to bilingualism in childhood and ways in which their bilingualism is perceived and valued in different ways. This chapter highlights what I see as most salient and also most problematic in the study of bilingual children. Any research into the bilingual development of children must not only entail the linguistic, pragmatic and cognitive development of children but also needs to be firmly rooted in its social and cultural context. However, as we shall see, much of the available research on childhood bilingualism is limited in scope – for example, studies often treat children's bilingualism as purely a phenomenon of language acquisition and give little regard to the social context in which the two languages are acquired (De Houwer, 1995; Genesee, 1989). In addition, few studies precisely describe their subjects' linguistic history or exposure patterns, which are necessary for cross-study comparisons (Schieffelin, 1994).

These difficulties notwithstanding, in the rest of this chapter, I outline the theoretical frameworks that have provided the foundations for the study of Korean American children. First, I discuss some of the common myths around being bilingual and establish a definition of bilingualism that I shall use throughout this book. Then I will review the research that illustrates the interactional value of codeswitching and introduce the sequential framework which will be used in the analysis of the Korean American children's language mixing. I review issues related to language acquisition by children who are exposed to two languages simultaneously from birth (i.e. 'simultaneous acquisition') and by children who are subsequently exposed to the second language later in childhood (i.e. 'successive acquisition'). Related to language acquisition, I discuss language socialization of bilingual children and how language development is influenced by the attitude of family members and school personnel toward the two languages in the child's linguistic repertoire. There is also a brief review of research on bilingual education and the controversies surrounding dual-language education of linguistic minority children. Research findings that emphasize the need for native-language development and maintenance by language minority children will be reviewed. Along this line, I discuss factors that contribute to language shift in the immigrant family and the costs associated with the loss of the heritage language. But first, I turn to a definition of bilingualism.

Definition of Bilingualism

Before embarking on a study of bilingual children, it is necessary to discuss what constitutes bilingualism in individuals. However, the task of defining who is and is not a bilingual is not as simple as it may at first appear. For example, one might reasonably argue that a bilingual is someone who can speak two languages. However, this definition is problematic for a number of reasons. How well should the person speak each of the languages to be considered bilingual? Can we consider someone who is just starting to learn a second language and who, therefore, knows only a few words in the second language bilingual? Is there an absolute minimal proficiency in the second language required in order for someone to qualify as a bilingual? Is a bilingual someone who has equal competence in both languages? But what exactly is meant by equal competence in two languages? What about someone who can understand a second language perfectly but cannot speak it? What about a person who can speak a second language but cannot read it? Can we rely on self-ratings of bilingual competence or should individuals be tested along certain standard measures? Is language proficiency the only criterion for assessing bilingualism or should the circumstances in which the two languages are used also be considered? For example, if a person has strictly separate uses of two languages (e.g. uses one language at work or in school and speaks the other language at home), can s/he be considered a bilingual?

Much of the early literature on bilingualism in the 1950s and 1960s is concerned with the issue of objectively measuring bilingualism in quantitative terms (see Kelly [1969]); see also Romaine [1995] for a summary). Psychologists have used a variety of tests to assess the relative dominance of one language over another. For example, Macnamara (1969) grouped the kinds of tests used to measure bilingual ability into four categories: rating scales, fluency tests, flexibility tests and dominance tests. Rating scales include instruments like language-usage scales, self-rating scales and interviews. In order to obtain a measurement of speakers' self-rating, individuals would be asked to assess their ability in a language in relation to various skills. A balance score is calculated by subtracting the values obtained for one language from those of the other. If the difference is close to zero or zero, the person is considered to be a balanced bilingual. Another kind of language self-assessment is done through the language diary, in which speakers are asked to keep track of the languages they use every day (see Romaine, 1983).

Fluency has generally been given much attention in proficiency rating. A variety of fluency tests have been used to assess language dominance, such as picture naming, word completion, oral reading and following instructions. Lambert (1955) developed a task in which subjects were asked to respond to instructions in both languages. Their response time was taken as an indication of whether they were balanced or dominant in one language. It was assumed that a balanced bilingual should take more or less the same amount of time to respond to instructions in both languages. However, such quantitative measures of the degree of bilingualism often overlook the more qualitative differences in language proficiency such as the individual's linguistic background and patterns of bilingual use in different settings. Romaine (1995) argues that the notion of balanced bilingualism is a mythical one, an artifact of a theoretical perspective that takes the monolingual speaker as its point of reference (for further discussions, see Baker & Prys Jones, 1998; Li, 2000: 5–8).

Is a bilingual two monolinguals in one person?

One of the widely held myths about bilingualism is that a bilingual is a sum of two monolinguals. Zentella (1997: 270) describes this mythical bilingual as 'two monolinguals joined at the neck'. It is often assumed that 'true bilinguals' are those who are equally fluent in their two languages, with proficiency in both languages comparable to those of monolinguals of those languages. In reality, however, bilinguals will rarely have balanced competence in their two languages. Terms such as 'full bilingual' and 'balanced bilingual' represent idealized concepts that do not characterize the great majority of the world's bilinguals. Rarely will any bilingual be equally proficient in speaking, listening, reading or writing both languages across all different situations and domains. However, the monolingual view of bilingualism is so entrenched in popular and scholarly thinking that bilinguals themselves may apologize to monolinguals for not speaking their language as well as the monolinguals do, thus accepting and reinforcing the myth.

In educational circles, the term 'semilingual' has been used to describe bilingual students who appear to lack proficiency in both languages (Martin-Jones & Romaine, 1986; Valadez *et al.*, 2000). Tests that are designed for monolinguals are often used to compare bilinguals' proficiency in either of their languages with that of monolinguals of those languages. These assessments often do not take into account the fact that bilinguals use their two languages with different people, in different contexts and for different purposes. The 'semilingual' view holds that there will be negative consequences for cognitive processing for bilinguals, because of the potential confusion between what monolinguals perceive as two underdeveloped languages.[2] For example, immigrant parents are routinely advised by doctors, speech therapists, teachers and counselors to forbid any other language, apart from English, to be used in their home so as not to 'confuse' the children with input from two languages (see Crepin-Lanzarotto, 1997; see also Chapter 6). However, the argument that bilingual input confuses children is not substantiated since most children growing up in bilingual or multilingual societies learn to use two or more languages with no apparent negative consequences to their cognitive development. Neither is this view supported by empirical social and psycholinguistic evidence.

So who is a bilingual? Grosjean (1985) presents a sociolinguistically sound definition of a bilingual, which I will adopt in this book:

> The bilingual is a fully competent speaker/hearer; he or she has developed competencies (in the two languages and possibly a third system that is a combination of the two) to the extent required by his or her needs and those of the environment. The bilingual uses the two languages – separately or together – for different purposes in different domains of life and with different people. Because the needs and uses of the two languages are usually quite different, the bilingual is rarely equally or completely fluent in the two languages. Levels of fluency in a language will depend on the need for that language and will be extremely domain specific. Because the bilingual is a human communicator (as is the monolingual) he or she has developed communicative competence that is sufficient for everyday life. This competence will make use of one language, or the other language (in the form of mixed speech) depending on the situation, topic, the interlocutor etc.'

Grosjean's definition emphasizes that bilingualism must be understood in its own right and that monolingual competence should not be used as a basis for assessing bilingual ability (see also, Grosjean, 1989). Since the bilingual uses the two languages for different purposes in different circumstances, s/he is rarely equally competent in both languages. One language is usually more dominant than the other in different situations or stages of life.

Communicative Value of Codeswitching

One of the ways in which children and adults display their bilingual abilities is through codeswitching, a change of language within a conversation, usually when bilinguals are in the company of other bilinguals. Codeswitching is perhaps the most obvious indication of one's bilingual abilities, since very few bilinguals keep their two languages completely separate (Baker & Prys Jones, 1998). However, monolinguals who hear bilinguals codeswitch may have negative attitudes toward codeswitching and think that it represents a lack of mastery of either language and an impure form of language. Bilinguals themselves may feel embarrassed about their codeswitching and attribute it to careless language habits or laziness (Grosjean, 1982: 148). Codeswitching is often given pejorative names such as 'Spanglish' or 'Tex–Mex' (mixture of Spanish and English by bilingual speakers in the American Southwest) and 'Franglais' (mixture of French and English in parts of French-speaking Canada). In classroom contexts, codeswitching is often discouraged by teachers who think that allowing students to talk in their first language is distracting and robs them of the opportunities to speak English. However, a great deal of research in the past few decades has shown that codeswitching, far from being a communicative deficit, is a valuable linguistic strategy (e.g. De Mejia, 1998; Gumperz, 1982; McClure, 1981; Milroy & Muysken, 1995; Moffatt & Milroy, 1992; Myers-Scotton, 1993; Poplack, 1980; Romaine, 1995; Shin & Milroy, 2000; Timm, 1975; Zentella, 1997).

Perhaps most notable in this regard, Gumperz (1982) argues that codeswitching is a discourse mode or a communicative option, available to a bilingual speaker in much the same way that switching between styles or dialects is an option for the monolingual speaker. Gumperz's work on bilingual interactive strategies contributed greatly to the field of bilingualism by directly contradicting the view that codeswitching represents a deficient knowledge of language, a grammarless mish-mash of two languages. According to Gumperz, codeswitching is a communicative resource that builds on the participants' perception of two contrasting languages and conveys linguistic and social information to other participants in the conversation. In addition, codeswitching indicates the speaker's momentary attitudes, communicative intents and emotions (see also Gal, 1979).

Under the heading of 'conversational codeswitching', Gumperz describes the strategies speakers use to choose their language. From this perspective, codeswitching is 'an element in a socially agreed matrix of contextualization cues and conventions used by speakers to alert addressees, in the course of ongoing interaction, to the social and situational context of the conversation' (Gumperz, 1982: 132–52). Therefore, through codeswitching, speakers communicate metaphoric information about how they intend their words to be understood by other participants (Gumperz, 1982: 61). Gumperz derives the conversational meaning of codeswitching through a sequential analysis, in which the language choice in one utterance is compared against the language choice in the preceding utterance. Following this approach, Gumperz (1982: 75–84) lists the following discourse functions of codeswitching:

(a) quotations (reported speech)
(b) addressee specification
(c) interjections
(d) reiteration
(e) message qualification
(f) personalization *versus* objectivization.

An example of how codeswitching contextualizes quotations (reported speech) is found in Romaine's (1995: 162) example of a young Papua New Guinean girl narrating the story of a cartoon she has just seen on the video. While the girl narrated the story in Tok Pisin, she reported the speech of one of the characters in English: Lapun man ia kam na tok, 'OH YU POOR PUSIKET', na em go insait [The old man came and said, 'Oh you poor pussycat', and then he went inside]. Romaine notes that the girl's switch to English here is socially appropriate because the cartoon characters are white and the setting is obviously not Papua New Guinea. It would, therefore, have been highly unlikely that the man in the cartoon would know Tok Pisin, which explains why the girl used English to quote him directly.

An example of codeswitching used for reiteration is found in a conversation of two Korean girls working on a classroom activity in the current study (see Appendixes 1 and 2 for a list of full Abbreviations and Transcription Conventions).

1	**Yooni:**	CAN I USE YOUR ERASER? /		
2	**Grace:**	(1.5)		
3	**Yooni:**	*Na*	ERASER	*sse-to-toy?*[3] /
		I	eraser	use-even-okay
		(Is it okay if I use your eraser?)		
4	**Grace:**	*Ne*	*iss-cyanha*	*keki* *ey/*
		You	have not	there LOC
		(You have it over there).		

Here, Yooni asks to borrow Grace's eraser even though she has her own. In the absence of a response from Grace (as shown by the 1.5-second silence), Yooni switches to Korean to repeat her request. This codeswitch is significant because it serves to emphasize and clarify Yooni's initial request. Yooni may have interpreted Grace's lack of response as a sign of misunderstanding or an intentional rejection of her request. Had Yooni been a monolingual English speaker, she may have repeated her request in English in a louder voice, perhaps also pointing her finger to the eraser to get Grace's attention. What is important to remember is that bilingual speakers have the option of switching to the other language, in addition to all of the things that monolinguals do (such as speaking in a louder voice and using gesture) to get their intended meanings across. Codeswitching, therefore, is an additional communicative strategy available to bilingual speakers.

Gumperz's analysis of codeswitching as interactional strategies is further developed by Scotton (1976, 1980, 1982, 1983) and particularly by Myers-Scotton's (1993) 'markedness' theory of language choice. Basing her arguments chiefly on East African bilingual conversational materials, she argues that bilingual speakers are innately endowed with a knowledge of socially relevant markedness which is associated with the normative and expected practices in a given community. This entails an awareness by competent speakers of the social consequences of choosing a particular language (or opting to mix languages) in a particular social context. Thus, while the unmarked choice in any context is the normatively expected one, speakers who make marked (i.e. unexpected or unusual) choices in specific contexts are responsible for the implicatures triggered by these choices. Readers are directed to Myers-Scotton (1993) for details of this influential and suggestive theory. Although it is claimed to be both comprehensive and predictive, capable of associating the social symbolism of particular languages with the conversational strategies of speakers, Myers-Scotton's theory presents difficulties in that it is not always clear how specific analyses can be supported or refuted; in particular, it is difficult to determine which languages become marked or unmarked in a given bilingual interaction. However, the idea of particular language choices being (un)marked in classroom discourse is a useful one to which I will return in Chapter 4.

Auer (1984, 1991, 1995) represents a very different development of Gumperz's interactional paradigm. Critical of Gumperz's characterization of speakers' linguistic choices as realizations of a pre-established set of functions (such as addressee selection, to mark emphasis or interjections), Auer argued that not only was such a list theoretically problematic and unmotivated but it could also never be complete in principle. Developing

Gumperz's idea of codeswitching as a contextualization cue, he suggested that the problems posed by an analysis in terms of functions could be solved by adopting the sequential framework of Conversation Analysis. As procedures for organizing the ongoing interaction, conversational participants appear to exploit variable spoken language elements at all linguistic levels (for further details see Li & Milroy, 1995). Auer's suggestion was that codeswitching worked much like other (for example) prosodic or gestural contextualization cues, the chief function of which is to signal participants' orientation to each other. For instance, while a particular utterance may be contextualized by its prosodic shape as ironical or mocking or as a side-sequence outside the current topic, the same job could be done by codeswitching. Auer argued that since the contrast set up by codeswitching was particularly visible, switching served as a particularly salient contextualization cue in bilingual communities.

Auer drew a useful distinction between participant-related switching (motivated by the language preferences or competence of participants) and discourse-related switching (setting up a contrast which structures some part of the discourse – e.g. reiteration of an utterance for emphasis in a different language). Auer points out that the discourse functions of codeswitching have received a great deal of attention in the existing literature, while processes of language negotiation and preference-influenced or competence-influenced language choices are usually not subsumed under conversational codeswitching but are considered to be either determined by societal macro-structures or psycholinguistic factors. The distinction which he draws between discourse- and participant-related codeswitching allows language alternation of all kinds to be discussed within a single framework.

To study codeswitching as a contextualization cue requires the analyst to focus on the sequential development of interaction, because the meanings of contextualization cues unfold as interaction proceeds and cannot be discussed without referring to the conversational context. The framework provided by Conversation Analysis (CA) is appropriate for this kind of analysis (see Atkinson & Heritage, 1984; Levinson, 1983: Chapter 6). In Auer's view, the CA approach has at least two advantages. First, it gives priority to 'the sequential implicativeness of language choice in conversation, that is, the fact that whatever language a participant chooses for the organization of his or her turn, or for an utterance which is part of the turn, the choice exerts an influence on subsequent language choices by the same or other speakers' (Auer, 1984: 5). Second, it 'limits the external analysts' interpretational leeway because it relates his or her interpretations back to the members' mutual understanding of their utterances as manifest in their behavior' (Auer, 1984: 6). It is this kind of sequential analysis, which I apply in my own analysis of the Korean American children's codeswitching in Chapter 4. Readers interested in a more in-depth explanation and application of Auer's framework may wish to refer to a recent collection of papers by Auer (1998), as well as Li (1994; 2002) and Shin and Milroy (2000), among other works.

Bilingual Acquisition

The development of childhood bilingualism cannot be discussed without referring to the language acquisition literature. In the following, I briefly review the processes underlying two main types of language acquisition by bilingual children: simultaneous and successive. I shall adopt McLaughlin's (1978) distinction between simultaneous and successive bilingual acquisition – a child who acquires two languages more or less from infancy is regarded as acquiring them simultaneously, whereas a child who is exposed to one language in infancy and the second language later in childhood (after the age of about three) is considered as acquiring the two languages successively. Children who acquire two languages simultaneously may do so because the father and the mother each speak a different language to the children. In contrast, linguistic minority children most often fit in the latter category – they acquire their first language in the home and immediate community and are regularly exposed to their second language when they enter school. It is important to note that 'successive acquisition' usually refers to cases in which the acquisition of the second language occurs through natural interaction with the native speakers of that language, unlike the artificial learning of the 'foreign' language in the context of the classroom (Klein, 1986).

Simultaneous bilingual acquisition

The earliest systematic studies of simultaneous acquisition of two languages were those by Ronjat (1913) and Leopold (1939–49), who raised their children bilingually. Ronjat introduced the "one person–one language" principle as the most effective method for raising a child bilingually in a home where the parents have different mother tongues. Following this approach, Leopold studied the acquisition of English and German by his daughter Hildegard by keeping a diary of Hildegard's speech until she became two years old. In the home, Leopold spoke only German to his wife and Hildegard, while his wife spoke only English. Leopold claims that Hildegard had one linguistic system (i.e. did not separate the two languages) and did not associate the languages with specific persons even though her parents spoke to her in different languages.

Leopold reports that it was only in her third year that Hildegard began to treat the two languages as separate linguistic systems and was able to translate between them.

Following Leopold, much research on simultaneous bilingual language acquisition has tried to determine whether a young bilingual child starts out with a single linguistic system or two separate linguistics systems from the beginnings of speech production. Perhaps the single most influential work on this question has been the study by Volterra and Taeschner (1978), which argued for a three-stage model of early bilingual development. As its name implies, this model portrays bilingual language development as progressing from a stage of initially mixed lexicon ("Stage I") to two separate lexical systems with one grammar ("Stage II"), which eventually becomes two fully separated lexical and grammatical systems ("Stage III"). However, this model has attracted significant criticism and there now seems to be a consensus in the field that the three-stage model does not accurately explain the bilingual acquisition process (see De Houwer, 1995; Paradis & Genesee, 1996).

The criticisms directed at the three-stage model have mainly concentrated on the first two components, which together constitute what is known as the "single system hypothesis" (see also Redlinger & Park, 1980; Vihman, 1985). Based on two children's (ages 1:10 and 1:6) performance, Volterra and Taeschner claim that, in 'Stage I', the words used in one language have no equivalent meaning that correspond to the words in the other language (i.e. the bilingual child is claimed to have a single, undifferentiated system). However, as De Houwer (1995) points out, Volterra and Taeschner's study has some methodological problems, which make their claims unconvincing. First, Volterra and Taeschner's list of 137 words is hardly adequate to decide whether a particular word item was being used as a translation equivalent of another term. Another problem is that the evidence for "Stage I" ultimately depends on the absence of certain forms rather than their presence. In addition, Volterra and Taeschner's data are not analyzed in relation to the sociolinguistic contexts in which they occurred (see also Genessee, 1989) – although the authors report that their subjects interacted with a German-speaking interlocutor, it is still possible that translation equivalents might have turned up in recorded conversations with an Italian-speaking interlocutor.

Research evidence has now been growing in favor of the hypothesis that a child's two languages develop separately from the very beginnings of speech production. Several studies have shown that bilingual children use the two grammars differently as soon as there is evidence of grammar (Döpke, 1997; Paradis & Genesee, 1996; Pfaff, 1992, 1994). Furthermore, the claim that bilingual children start out with a single, undifferentiated lexicon is challenged by recent studies that show that bilingual children have a fairly stable rate of translation equivalents (words used in one language that correspond to words with equivalent meaning in the other language) as soon as they begin talking (Pearson *et al.*, 1995; Quay, 1995). In addition, there is now evidence that bilingual children acquire pragmatic knowledge even before showing lexical differentiation (Nicoladis, 1998).

Successive bilingual acquisition

Unlike simultaneous bilingual acquisition, studies on successive bilingual acquisition have often been carried out in the field of second-language acquisition (see Klein, 1986; Larsen-Freeman & Long, 1991; Gass & Selinker, 2001 for introductory literature). However, second-language acquisition research has traditionally dealt more with adult language acquisition than with child language acquisition (Romaine, 1995) and there is currently a severe shortage of systematic studies available in successive bilingual acquisition in childhood.

Much of the research on successive language acquisition by children has focused on whether young learners use similar linguistic and cognitive strategies in the acquisition of a first and a second language. Following Brown's (1973) finding that there is a common, invariant sequence of acquisition for at least 14 bound morphemes by children acquiring English as their native language, several researchers have examined the developmental sequences followed by children acquiring English as a second language. These studies attempt to determine whether the sequence found by Brown is also found in children acquiring English as a second language and whether children of different first-language backgrounds acquire grammatical morphemes in the same sequence. While some scholars claim that the first language (L1) and the second language (L2) developmental sequences are similar (e.g. Ravem, 1968, 1974; Milon, 1974; Dato, 1970; Ervin-Tripp, 1974), others argue that L2 child learners operate in a manner more similar to adult L2 learners than to children acquiring a first language (e.g. Wode, 1976, 1978; Cancino *et al.*, 1974, 1975; Hakuta, 1976).

More recently, researchers working in the tradition of Universal Grammar (UG) have proposed various theories of L1 and L2 processing. Specifically, a number of rationalist approaches to second-language acquisition have assumed *fundamental differences* in L1 and L2 acquisition (e.g. Felix, 1984; Clahsen, 1990; Meisel, 1991; Bley-Vroman, 1990). These scholars claim that while L1 learners have access to UG, L2 learners do not. Other researchers, however, argue that L1 and L2 acquisition processes are similar and that adult L2 learners have access to UG (e.g. Vainikka & Young-

Scholten, 1994; Schwartz & Sprouse, 1994; White, 1989). At present, however, the central issues in this debate are difficult to resolve, chiefly because this research has made little use of relevant contemporary research in cognitive science and neuroscience (see Carroll, 1998; Schachter, 1998).

Aside from comparing L1 and L2 developmental sequences, some studies, especially those concerned with L2 pedagogy, have taken up the question of whether common developmental sequences are found in L2 learners with different L1 backgrounds. Comparing one group of Spanish-speaking children learning English and another group of Chinese-speaking children learning English, aged six to eight, Dulay and Burt (1973, 1974) found that both groups exhibited significantly related accuracy ordering of 11 English bound morphemes elicited using the Bilingual Syntax Measure (BSM), a picture-elicitation device using colored cartoons.[4] Given the very different grammars of Chinese and Spanish, Dulay and Burt argued that universal language-processing strategies are the basis for the child's organization of an L2, and that it is the L2 system, rather than the L1 system, that guides the acquisition of the L2. Several studies of adult English learners using the BSM (e.g. Bailey *et al.*, 1974; Larsen-Freeman, 1975) also indicate that despite differences in amount of instruction, exposure to English and first language, there is a high degree of agreement as to the relative difficulty of the set of grammatical morphemes studied (see Larsen-Freeman & Long (1991: 88–92) for a review of subsequent morpheme studies done using different data collection and analysis procedures). Zobl and Liceras (1994) drew similar conclusions from their analysis of earlier studies of English L1 and L2 morpheme acquisition orders based on a functional-categories framework.

However, some research on English morpheme acquisition does not support the conclusion of a universal order of acquisition among all L2 learners. Hakuta and Cancino (1977) have argued that the semantic complexity of the morphemes varies according to the learner's native language. They claim that an L2 learner whose first language does not make the same discriminations as the target-language experience more difficulty in learning to use these morphemes than learners whose L1 makes the semantic discrimination. For example, Hakuta's (1976) Japanese-speaking child experienced great difficulty with the definite/indefinite contrast – Japanese being a language that does not mark this distinction in the same way as English. Similarly, Vainikka and Young-Scholten (1994) argued that the sequence of acquisition of German phrase structure by adult Korean and Turkish learners of German is influenced by their L1.

Hakuta (1976) also showed that the acquisition order of his Japanese subject was very different from that of Dulay and Burt's (1974) Chinese-speaking and Spanish-speaking subjects. Similarly, Pak (1987), who employed BSM elicitation procedures, showed that the order of English grammatical morpheme acquisition of a group of Korean-speaking children living in Texas was significantly different from that of Dulay and Burt's (1974) subjects. These studies provide a basis for examining the Korean children's morphological developmental patterns. In Chapter 5, I compare my own data in turn with those of Brown's (1973) monolingual English-speaking subjects, Dulay and Burt's (1974) Chinese- and Spanish-speaking children, Hakuta's (1976) Japanese-speaking child and Pak's (1987) Korean children to assess the extent of similarities and differences among the acquisition orders of the various groups.

The question of whether L1 and L2 developmental sequences are the same where young children acquire two languages successively has been addressed in research with Turkish children in Germany and in The Netherlands (e.g. Pfaff, 1992, 1993, 1994; Boeschoten, 1990; Verhoeven, 1988; Verhoeven & Boeschoten, 1986; Verhoeven and Vermeer, 1985). These studies analyze the grammatical errors made by bilingual children in each language and compare them to the errors made by age-equivalent monolingual speakers of those languages. Their conclusion is that bilingual children lag behind monolingual children in their development of both languages. For example, Pfaff (1993) studied the successive bilingual development of Turkish immigrant children in Germany and found that the German-dominant bilingual children made more errors in Turkish than did Turkish-dominant bilingual children. Compared to monolingual Turkish children who acquire finite and non-finite gerunds in Turkish by 2 years of age (Slobin, 1988), the German-dominant bilingual children in Pfaff's study did not have gerund forms in their speech.

In another study of Turkish immigrant children, this one in The Netherlands, Verhoeven (1988) found that his Turkish–Dutch bilingual subjects also used very few gerunds in Turkish. There were only three occurrences of participles and gerunds in narratives by eight children at age 8. Boeschoten's (1990) study also found a general lack of gerund use among Turkish–Dutch bilingual children – of the 12 subjects, aged 4 through 6, only five used any gerund forms at all, while all used adverbials. However, Verhoeven's subjects made extensive use of adverbials that are typically found in the speech of 5-year-old monolingual children in Turkey. Verhoeven suggests that the use of adverbials is a "compensation strategy" which helps achieve their communicative goals. Verhoeven also suggests that the bilingual children's developmental delay is related to restricted Turkish input in the Dutch-speaking environment.

While the Turkish–German and Turkish–Dutch bilingual children fall behind in their development of Turkish, the Turkish produced by the children is, nonetheless, relatively error-free compared to their German, which seems to present far more difficulty for the immigrant children (Pfaff, 1994). For example, Pfaff found that even the German-dominant bilingual children in her study made many errors in German, resembling patterns of L2 acquisition of German observed for adults and older children than patterns of L1 acquisition of German by monolingual children. Similarly, Verhoeven and Vermeer (1985) found that their Turkish–Dutch bilingual subjects fall behind Dutch monolingual children in their development of Dutch. They argue that just as restricted Turkish input is linked to a developmental lag in Turkish, restricted German or Dutch input is related to the children's lag in German or Dutch development.

The finding that the bilingual children lag behind monolingual children in grammatical development in both languages (even if temporarily) may not be all that surprising. Since a bilingual develops competencies in the two languages to the extent required by his/her communicative needs, and since the needs and uses of the two languages are usually quite different (e.g., one language for school, another for home), a bilingual is rarely fully proficient in both languages. However, many researchers and practitioners have mistaken (temporary) delayed development in both languages as evidence that bilingualism hurts immigrant children and have advocated for the use of one language (usually the school language, or the language of the society). Bilingual children cannot be expected to show proficiencies in both languages that are equal to those of their same-age monolingual peers at all times.

More significantly, however, the social context in which these Turkish children acquire their two languages may be of central importance in our understanding of the results. The Turkish immigrant children in these studies live in largely urban areas with high concentrations of Turkish immigrants of low socioeconomic backgrounds. Although Pfaff's subjects attend a 'bilingual' day-care program where half of the teaching staff speaks German and the other half Turkish, the aim of these programs can hardly be said to promote functional bilingualism. In fact, this type of program is an example of 'guest-worker education', where Turkish children (who account for more than 90% of the student population in the day-care program in Pfaff's study) are segregated from mainstream German children for the purpose of mother-tongue instruction so that they can eventually return to their homeland (Clyne, 1984; Skutnabb-Kangas, 1984a, 1984b).

Skutnabb-Kangas (2000: 587–592) observes that while such segregation programs give the children at least some chance of learning their native language to some extent, these do not make them high-level bilinguals. Indeed, the teachers may be bilingual but are often poorly trained and the schools have poorer facilities and fewer resources than schools for dominant-group children. The teaching of German as an L2 is poor (or non-existent) and culturally appropriate teaching materials are often in short supply. In addition, opportunity to practice the L2 in peer-group contexts outside school is very much lacking and students often suffer from anxiety, low self-confidence and low teacher expectations. Skutnabb-Kangas (2000: 579) notes that even with a great deal of effort in the family and the community, many of the minority children in these 'subtractive non-forms of bilingual education' become virtually monolingual in the majority language.

Contextual information such as this is critically missing in the majority of childhood bilingual acquisition studies. Since only a few studies precisely describe subjects' linguistic history and exposure patterns, as well as the social context of acquisition, it is difficult to make cross-study comparisons (see also Schieffelin, 1994; De Houwer, 1995). Thus, the available research provides an inadequate basis for answering many of the important questions such as, "Why do some children develop into bilinguals while others become monolingual in the dominant language?" Socially and culturally detailed accounts of bilingual acquisition are prerequisites for understanding the language development of linguistic minority children. In this regard, research in language socialization holds much promise in illuminating the contextual circumstances in which the two languages are learned and used.

Language Attitude and Socialization

In any bilingual situation, there is typically an unequal distribution of power that is represented by the languages in question. By interacting with members of their family, school and community, children learn that one language may be valued more than another and decide to become more proficient in that language. The highly valued language has a better chance of survival as part of a young child's individual linguistic repertoire as well as part of the community's repertoire over time (Ochs & Schieffelin, 1995). For example, in many Native American communities, young people are lured by educational and economic opportunities that their English skills can bring and often do not see the value of learning and maintaining their heritage language. In the state of California, of approximately 150 indigenous languages spoken at the time the Europeans arrived, only 50 are still spoken today, most only by elders; and virtually 100% of California's indigenous languages are no longer learned by children (Hinton, 1994). The situation is made worse by the fact that, in many cases, the indigenous language is not only devalued but also extensively stigmatized.

Cummins (1996) notes that prior to the 1970s, it was extremely common for teachers to reprimand bilingual students for speaking their home language in the school. Separating minority children from their parents and sending them to boarding schools has been a common practice in most parts of the world (Skutnabb-Kangas, 2000). Minority children have been taken from their families, sent to boarding schools in distant areas and punished when caught speaking their native languages. All too often, the message communicated to students is that they must no longer identify with their native language and culture, which are deemed objectionable in the school and society. In her study of children of migrant workers in the United States, Lopez (1999: 193) describes how language minority children are pressured to choose between the language of the school and their native language:

> School has a way of positioning marginalized students against their families so that there has to be a choice of one or the other. This type of dichotomy destroys family discourse interaction for the children who want to succeed in school. It is most destructive when a student is also forced to choose a dominant language that is different from the home language as a result of embracing the dominant discourse. Are we to assume that the only way for minority children to get ahead in life is to renounce everything that they have come to know and love about their primary discourse?

As perhaps the single most powerful socializing institution in children's lives, the school imparts cultural knowledge and practices to its students and serves as the first step toward assimilation of linguistic minority children into the Anglo-American society. Language socialization at school takes place explicitly, as teachers instruct students on what to say and how to say things, as well as indirectly in teachers' interaction with students (Heath, 1983). Once language minority children enter school, they quickly realize that the language they speak with their family members has no appreciable value in school and that they need to learn English to be accepted by their teachers and peers (Wong Fillmore, 1991). The school endorses mainstream, middle-class values and children who do not come to school with the kind of linguistic and cultural background supported in the schools are likely to experience conflict (Romaine, 1995: 242). Children are, therefore, motivated to learn English, while, at the same time, motivated to discontinue using their primary languages. This motivation is often the initial driving force in familial language shift, as children start speaking English to their parents and siblings at home. As the children learn and use English at home, the parents also switch over to it. Parents often learn enough English to carry on simple conversations with their children and their English abilities may improve overtime, albeit slowly. This may explain why many studies of different immigrant communities report that length of residence in the US correlates significantly with the amount of English spoken by parents (e.g. Harres, 1989; Li, 1982; Shin, 2002a; Sridhar, 1988; Young & Tran, 1999).

Besides the school, however, the ethnic family and community play an important role in socializing children to use language. For example, in his study of the Gapun community of Papua New Guinea, Kulick (1992) found that the local vernacular Taiap is quickly disappearing from the linguistic repertoire of children, not because of an explicit devaluation of Taiap but because of implicit devaluation through language socialization practices in the family. Taiap adults insist that they want children to acquire Taiap and place the blame for its loss on children's reluctance to learn it. However, in reality, Taiap adults codeswitch into Tok Pisin far more than they realize and socialize young children into associating Tok Pisin with modernity, Christianity and education and Taiap with backwardness and paganism. Children, therefore, come to understand that Tok Pisin is the more desirable language and speak it more and more, while using less and less Taiap.

Another example of how language ideology affects bilingual acquisition is found in Schieffelin's (1994) study of Haitian families in New York City. Although young children in these families speak in Haitian Creole, English and sometimes French, they mostly use English. While adults assume that all Haitian children automatically learn to speak Creole since they have a Haitian heritage, they think that explicit instruction is required for English, which is seen as essential for academic work and for successful participation in American society. Haitian adults are found to use Creole to praise children when the children speak in English and even to codeswitch to paraphrase their own and children's utterances in English. These language socialization practices in the family convey to Haitian children that English is the more important language. However, this should not be taken to mean that immigrant parents do not want children to retain their mother tongue. As we shall see in Chapter 6, there are enormous economic and societal pressures on minority parents to encourage the use of English by their children. Educational policies regarding the language of instruction for language minority children in particular, contribute considerably to language socialization practices, to which I now turn.

Bilingual Education: Transitional *versus* Maintenance

The term 'bilingual education' can mean different things in different contexts. This is because bilingual education programs can be categorized into different types depending on program goals, status of the student group (e.g. dominant/subordinated, majority/minority etc.), proportion of instructional time spent in each language, and sociolinguistic and sociopolitical situation in the immediate community and wider society (see Cummins, [1996], Hornberger, [1991] and Skutnabb-Kangas, [1984a] for a review). Hornberger (1991) shows how the same terms are often confusingly used for different types of educational programs and, conversely, different terms for the same type. For example, so-called transitional bilingual education is also referred to as compensatory or assimilation bilingualism. For the purpose of this book, I shall adopt Cummins' (1996) distinction of two broad types that can be defined either in terms of the *means* or in terms of the *goal* of a particular program.

When defined in terms of the *means*, bilingual education simply refers to the use of two (or more) languages of instruction to varying degrees in various instructional contexts and proficiency in two languages is not necessarily a desired outcome. For example, transitional bilingual programs aim to promote students' proficiency in the second language only. In this type of program, competence in two languages is not a desired goal. Snow and Hakuta (1992: 390) comment that, contrary to what the name suggests, the effect of many bilingual education programs in the United States is monolingualism in English: 'What it fosters is monolingualism; bilingual classrooms are efficient revolving doors between home-language monolingualism and English monolingualism.' As the most common form of bilingual education in the United States, transitional bilingual programs provide children with just enough L1 support to be mainstreamed into English only instruction. Once mainstreamed, students no longer receive L1 instruction and support. This policy persists in spite of the fact that research has shown that transitional bilingual education is associated with "lower levels of second language proficiency, scholastic underachievement, and psychosocial disorders" (Hakuta & Mostafapour, 1996: 42). I shall return to this point in the next section.

When defined in terms of *goals*, bilingual education can support the development of bilingual skills in children. When used in this sense, the delivery of instruction may actually take place exclusively in one language rather than two. For instance, immigrant students may be taught exclusively in their first languages for a period of time (say, from kindergarten to grades 2, 3 or 4) so that they can be exposed to maximum opportunity to learn those languages in social and academic contexts. This is done to help students establish proficiency in the minority language, which is weaker and lower in status than the language spoken by the majority population. French immersion programs across Canada and two-way bilingual education programs in the US are examples of such maintenance-oriented programs. After the initial grades, these programs maintain close to 50% of instruction in the minority language throughout elementary school. This type of program fosters 'additive bilingualism' (Lambert, 1977), in which an L2 is acquired with the expectation that the mother tongue will continue to be learned and used. Significant amount of support is provided to the development of the minority language by delivering instruction in the minority language.

Effects of Bilingual Education

Much of the policies regarding the education of language minority students in the United States have been driven by a major hypothesis called 'maximum exposure' (Cummins, 1996). The 'maximum exposure' hypothesis argues that if children lack proficiency in English, they require maximum exposure to English in school in order to learn it. This hypothesis has led to the claim that immersion in English is the most effective means to ensure the learning of English. It is also assumed that, under these conditions of immersion, language minority students will pick up sufficient English in about one or two years to survive academically without further special support. In addition, it is assumed that, in order for students to learn English quickly, English immersion should start as early as possible in the student's school career since younger children are better language learners than older children. Cummins (1996) notes that this hypothesis fails to account for the success of students enrolled in enrichment bilingual education programs (e.g. Canadian French immersion programs or two-way bilingual programs in the US). He notes that countless evaluations have shown that students in French immersion programs make good progress in acquiring French fluency and literacy at no cost to their English academic skills despite considerably less instructional time spent in English. Students in French immersion programs in Canada may lag behind their monolingual peers initially, but they catch up within a few years and may even surpass them (Swain & Lapkin, 1982).

The argument put forth by opponents of bilingual education that deficiencies in English should be remediated by intensive instruction in English seems to make much more sense than the argument that instruction in the native language helps promote English skills. This latter argument appears to be based on a "less equals more" type of logic that is unlikely to convince skeptics (Cummins, 1996). However, bilingual education advocates have consistently criticized transitional bilingual programs and have argued for enrichment bilingual programs that promote the development of literacy in two languages (e.g. Cummins, 1996; Fishman, 1976; Hornberger, 1998). They suggest that reinforcing children's conceptual base in their native language throughout elementary school (and beyond) will provide a foundation for long-term growth in English academic skills.

There is consistent evidence that strong support of bilingual students' first languages throughout elementary school contributes significantly to their academic success. A clear demonstration of the importance of promoting L1 literacy is provided by two large-scale studies involving children enrolled in bilingual education programs. A study by Ramirez (1992) involved 2,352 Latino elementary schoolchildren in nine school districts, 51 schools and 554 classrooms. He suggests that there is no direct relationship between the instructional time spent through the medium of a majority language and academic achievement in that language. On the contrary, there appears to be an inverse relation between exposure to English instruction and English achievement for Latino students in this study. An additional finding by Ramirez (1992) was that learning English language skills by immigrant students requires six or more years of special instructional support, a finding consistent with the results of other studies (e.g. Collier, 1987; Cummins, 1981).

In another study involving 42,000 bilingual students in five school districts in various regions of the United States, Thomas and Collier (2002) report that two-way enrichment bilingual education programs are the most successful in language minority students' long-term academic achievement, as measured by standardized tests across all the subject areas. As a group, students in this program maintain grade-level skills in their first language throughout their schooling and reach the 50th percentile in their second language after four to five years of schooling in both languages. The defining characteristics of such programs are:

(1) integrated schooling, with English speakers and language minority students learning each others' languages;
(2) perception among staff, students and parents that it is a "gifted and talented" program, leading to high expectations for student performance;
(3) equal status of the two languages, creating self-confidence among language minority students;

(4) healthy parent involvement among both language minority and English-speaking parents, for closer home–school cooperation; and

(5) continuous support for staff development emphasizing whole language, natural language acquisition through all content areas, cooperative learning, interactive and discovery learning and cognitive complexity for all proficiency levels.

Other evidence of the academic advantage gained by strong support of students' L1 can be seen in a study involving native Korean-speaking schoolchildren in the Los Angeles Unified School District (Sohn, n.d.). This study surveyed and tested native Korean-speaking students in three program types: (1) all-English, (2) modified bilingual, and (3) Korean/English dual-language program. Students in the all-English program received instruction through the fourth grade entirely in English. Students in the modified bilingual program received instruction mostly in English but also received Korean support. However, the modified bilingual program does not include development of Korean language literacy skills. Students in the dual-language program received instruction in both Korean and English in all curricular areas beginning in kindergarten.

Sohn found that students in the Korean–English dual-language program performed equally well in English language skills, as measured by standardized test scores (Stanford 9), as Korean children in all-English programs. She also found that students in dual-language programs scored higher in Korean language and general academic skills than those in modified bilingual programs. Based on these results, Sohn cautions that parents of children in all-English programs need to know that their children will not necessarily develop better English skills in an all-English program. The importance of this result cannot be overestimated since parents choose all-English programs precisely to help children acquire English more quickly. Sohn suggests that parents should be informed that learning Korean does not adversely affect the development of English.

Other evaluations of various bilingual education programs have consistently preferred models that allow children to develop their native language to high levels of proficiency while learning English (Shannon, 1999; Snow, 1990). Willig (1985) conducted a meta-analysis of 23 bilingual education programs in the United States. She found an overall advantage in both English and Spanish criterion tests for children who were in bilingual programs, although the size of the effect depended on such factors as the type of program and the academic domain of the criterion test. In sum, enrichment bilingual programs, whose aim is not only maintenance but also development and extension of the minority languages and cultural pluralism, offer much potential for both majority and minority learners' academic success (Hornberger, 1998: 449). In Chapter 7, I address the issue of educating parents and the community of the benefits of bilingualism and maintenance bilingual education and offer suggestions for successful acquisition of minority languages.

Effects of Bilingualism on the Child

A great deal of research has shown that there are many individual and societal benefits of bilingualism. For example, bilingualism develops cultural diversity in societies; it promotes ethnic identity and intergenerational relationships; it leads to social and cultural adaptability and adds to the mental health of the child (Baker & Prys Jones, 1998; Crystal, 1987). Becoming bilingual has cognitive advantages for the learner and results in superior scholastic achievement (Cummins, 1996; Krashen, 1998). A large number of studies (e.g. Bialystok, 2001; Cummins & Swain, 1986; Hakuta & Diaz, 1985), most of which investigated children's explicit knowledge about the structure and functions of language itself, have reported that bilingual children exhibit a greater sensitivity to linguistic meanings and may be more flexible in their thinking than monolingual children are. However, not all research shows the positive effects of bilingualism. Before 1960, there were an overwhelming number of studies that highlighted the negative effects of bilingualism on children (see Grosjean, 1982: 220–27; Romaine, 1995: 107). Observers noted many problems with language development of bilingual children, such as restricted vocabularies, limited grammatical structures, unusual word order, errors in morphology, hesitations, stuttering, and so on. Some have even argued that bilingualism could impair the child's intelligence and lead to split personalities. How can these contradictory findings be explained?

In a comparative analysis of selected studies, Swain and Cummins (1979) report that the positive effects are usually associated with language majority children in immersion programs, where knowledge of two languages is valued highly, where the children learn the L2 without losing the first and where the parents are of relatively high socioeconomic status. For example, middle-class English-speaking parents in Canada who enroll their children in French immersion programs choose to do so because of the perceived benefits of knowing another language. The educational goal of such programs is the enrichment of children from the dominant group through instruction in a second language. The children's L1 (English in this case) is respected and is in no danger of being replaced by the L2 (French). Teachers in immersion programs have high expectations for children's achievement and there is usually a significant level of parental involvement and support. French is considered a valuable addition to the children's existing linguistic repertoire and the most usual outcome is proficiency in both English and French. This type of bilingual development corresponds to Lambert's (1977) 'additive bilingualism'.

In contrast, negative effects are found with linguistic minority children who are forced to learn the majority language and are not encouraged to maintain their mother tongue and whose social environment does not induce learning. The bilingualism of linguistic minority children is different from that of linguistic majority children because the home language is not supported in school and the society. Minority children usually experience enormous pressures to learn the societal language and feel that they need to give up their L1 in order to be accepted by the mainstream society. In school, the bilingualism of linguistic minority children is considered a handicap, and children's prior linguistic and cultural knowledge is deemed irrelevant or undesirable. The message given by the educational and social establishments is that immigrants need to be rapidly integrated into the mainstream society, which entails abandoning the ethnic language and culture. It is small wonder why so many immigrant children end up losing their mother tongue and become monolingual in the societal language. This situation corresponds to Lambert's 'subtractive bilingualism'.

Language Shift and Maintenance

A substantial number of studies have documented shifts in language usage and attitude in various settings where the mother tongue is different from the socially and economically dominant language (e.g. De Klerk, 2000; Harres, 1989; Li, 1982; Putz, 1991; Sridhar, 1988; Taft & Cahill, 1989; Young & Tran, 1999). Language shift occurs when linguistic communities come in contact with a language that offers greater practical and economic rewards. Observations of different communities that come into contact with a majority language have shown that there is almost always a complete shift in language use within three generations barring any special effort (Fishman, 1989). In the usual scenario, the first generation speaks the native language, while the bilingual second generation comes between the native-language-speaking first generation and the majority language-speaking third generation.

However, recently, more and more language-minority communities are undergoing a complete shift in language within two generations with no intervening generation (Wiley, 2001). This obviously creates major communication problems, as parents and children living in the same household do not understand each other. This certainly is the case in many Korean

American homes where parents and children have frequent communication problems due to a lack of a common language. Language shift may be
slower in some communities where a large number of the same-language
speakers are concentrated in one area (e.g. Spanish in parts of the south-
western US). But invariably with the exception of a few cases (see Fishman,
1991), minority languages do not survive beyond the second or third
generation. The failure of the intergenerational transmission of the heritage
languages constitutes an enormous loss of foreign language resources to
individuals, communities and the nation as a whole (see also Krashen *et al.*
1998).

Language shift is often initiated when immigrant children begin
attending schools with a medium of instruction other than their mother
tongue and begin using the school language at home (Wong Fillmore,
1991). In many cases, children initiate language change in immigrant
homes but parents also variably accept and promote the use of the societal
language at home for various reasons (Richards & Yamada-Yamamoto,
1998; Tuominen, 1999). Some of these reasons may be internal – some
parents may choose to speak English because they do not want their children to feel "different" from mainstream children. Some parents may want
to distinguish themselves from more recent immigrants who tend to be
poorer and less accustomed to American ways of life. Other reasons may be
external – parents may be advised by teachers and childcare professionals
to speak English so as to maximize children's exposure to English. These
issues will be explored in detail in Chapter 6.

The Hidden Costs of Mother-Tongue Loss

What happens when immigrant children lose their native languages?
Loss of the heritage language by immigrant children can have highly
disruptive impact on family relations. For one, parents cannot express their
thoughts and feelings to their own children in the language of their heart:

> I am ashamed of my illiteracy of the English language. I used to say I
> came to the United States for my children's better education and their
> bright future. But frankly speaking, I have not spent enough time with
> them. I spend more time working. I thought it was best way for them. I
> mean, I thought financial support was a more important factor than
> anything else. I have a sixteen-year-old boy and a twelve-year-old girl. I
> came to the United States in 1977, when my son was two years old. After
> my son entered junior high school, I realized we had some gap between
> us. The gap was getting wider and wider because of a lack of communi-
> cation. I should have learned the English language or I should have

taught Korean to my children, but I did not do either. Now, I wonder why I came to the United States. For my children? Or for myself? (Quoted in Jo, 1999: 49)

Contrary to a popular assumption that immigrants do not want to learn English, immigrants themselves understand very well that learning English is not a luxury but a necessity. While immigrants in earlier days could labor on farms, work in factories and build railroads without speaking fluent English, today's service-oriented economy requires English ability for all but the lowest paying jobs (Tse, 2001). Lack of English skills is precisely what forces many immigrants to take multiple low-paying menial jobs. After working 12+ hours a day in physically demanding labor, it is difficult to spend quality time with children, let alone do anything as challenging as learning a new language. Free or low-cost English classes are often in short supply and parents face additional difficulties in finding childcare while they attend classes. Immigrant parents are driven by the desire to survive in the new country and do their best in difficult circumstances. However, too many handicapping conditions prevent them from doing all that they want to do as parents. Like the Korean mother in the previous example , many parents end up blaming themselves for not having done enough for their children.

In a study of Korean American college students, Cho and Krashen (1998) report that loss of Korean interfered with the students' ability to communicate with their parents. All of the subjects were either born in the US or came to the US before school age and reported that they spoke Korean fluently before entering elementary school. However, all of them report that they are now more comfortable in English and use English with their siblings and friends. The following excerpts from Cho and Krashen (1998: 33–36) provide poignant descriptions of their sense of frustration stemming from lack of competence in Korean:

My parents and I do have a communication gap, a communication problem. Not in just a sophisticated way. I can't even hold a normal conversation with my parents. I just say my thoughts once and I repeat it constantly until they understand.

I see barriers between my mom and my sister. I can explain what I want...like when my sister wants something, if she says it directly to my mom, my mom just doesn't get it, and they get frustrated with each other and they are like fighting, tension... I can just say 'Mom, this is what she meant and my mom says, 'Oh, why doesn't she say so...okay...go to the movie'.

It is frustrating when I'm speaking with my parents and we can't fully comprehend what we're trying to say to each other. I hate it when I eat dinner with my parents and they always carry on their own conversation that I can only half understand… I hate having something to say but not being able to say it

Breakdown in family communication can lead to the alienation of children from their parents and delinquency. However heritage-language development helps ensure strong parent–child communication and improve family relationships. Ensuring open and clear parent–child communication through investment in heritage language and culture is not only beneficial for the immigrant family and community but also constructive for the society at large. In Chapter 7, I make suggestions for successfully transmitting and maintaining heritage languages.

Summary

In this chapter, I have outlined the theoretical frameworks that have provided the foundations for this book. The study of bilingual children is necessarily multifaceted, with a multitude of linguistic, cognitive, social and educational factors contributing to the development of two or more languages. Contrary to popular thinking that a bilingual is two monolinguals in one person, a bilingual is rarely equally or completely fluent in the two languages. This is because the bilingual speaker uses his/her two languages for different purposes in different circumstances. Rather than using the monolingual as a yardstick against which a bilingual's proficiency in each language is measured and judged to fall short, one needs to consider a bilingual as a fully competent speaker who has developed adequate competences in the two languages for his or her particular communicative needs. Related to the idea of considering a bilingual to be a fully competent speaker is the notion of communicative value of codeswitching. Contrary to popular thinking that it is an impure, lazy and haphazard mixture of two languages, codeswitching is a valuable conversational tool for bilingual speakers to communicate their meanings.

Children's bilingual utterances and developmental patterns cannot be analyzed in isolation but must be interpreted in their proper social and cultural context. For example, studies that investigate children's successive acquisition of two languages during childhood conclude that immigrant children generally lag behind monolingual children in terms of grammatical development in both languages. However, in interpreting these results, one must take into account the larger social context in which the immigrant children are growing up, which systematically denigrates ethnic languages and cultures. Despite a great deal of research evidence that shows the positive impact of sustained native-language development on the academic achievement of language minority children, much of the educational programs for immigrant children are based on assimilation ideologies. In most programs, native-language support is only temporary and the underlying goal is acquisition of the majority language.

Each child's bilingualism is in a constant state of flux, influenced by a unique combination of socializing influences of the family, school and the community. As perhaps the single most powerful socializing institution in children's lives, the school serves to integrate language minority children into mainstream society. Children are quick to realize that their native language is not valued in school and that they must use English to be accepted by their teachers and peers. Children are discouraged from using their native languages and are motivated to speak only English, which may also be variably accepted and promoted by their parents and community. As children's English skills are continually improved and refined, their native languages dwindle from lack of use, eventually resulting in loss. Language loss in immigrant children is not only a loss for immigrant children but also for their families and the society. It is an absolute tragedy when parents and children cannot talk to one another due to a lack of a common language.

Chapter 2

Koreans in the United States

In order to understand the bilingual experiences of Korean American children it is important to begin with a description of their families, the history of their heritage, the languages they speak and the background to their settlement in the United States. This chapter sets out the context for the current study by outlining the social and economic backgrounds of the Korean immigrants who arrived in the United States in three major waves, focusing primarily on the most recent wave, which accounts for the vast majority of the present Korean population in the United States. I shall also describe the linguistic structure of the Korean language.

Korean Americans are among the more recent immigrant groups to enter American society, with over two-thirds of the present Korean population in the United States having arrived after 1970. There are over one million Koreans in the United States today and they rank fifth in number of the Asian and Pacific Islander population in the US after the Chinese, Filipino, Asian Indian and Vietnamese immigrants. These new immigrants from Korea are geographically more dispersed than other recent Asian immigrants but a substantial majority of them are concentrated in large metropolitan areas, such as Los Angeles, New York, Chicago and Washington, D.C. The typical Korean immigrant is young and married, with a preference for living in urban areas on either the West Coast or in the northeast, where there are high concentrations of Korean immigrants (Jo, 1999).

There are a good number of book-length descriptions of the historical, social, religious and economic issues concerning Koreans in America and readers interested in more in-depth discussions may wish to refer to them (e.g. Choe, 1980; Hurh, 1998; Hurh and Kim, 1984; Jo, 1999; Lee, 1991; Park, 1997). However, in this chapter, I can only discuss those aspects that are directly relevant to the understanding of the aspects of language use among Korean Americans. The subsequent sub-sections of this chapter deal in turn, with the following aspects of Korean Americans. First, I present a brief history of Korean immigration to the USA along with a review of the major factors that have influenced emigration. Next, I discuss the social and demographic characteristics of Koreans in the USA, focusing in turn on their education and occupation, social networks and language use. The future organization of Korean American communities will also be discussed in light of current immigration trends. Finally, I provide a description of the linguistic properties of Korean, comparing it where necessary to the structure of English.

A Brief History of Korean Immigration to the United States

The current composition of Korean immigrant populations in America is perhaps best understood from a historical perspective. Korea has nearly 2,000 years of written history, but until the turn of the 20th century it was known as the 'Hermit Kingdom of Asia.'[5] Korea was the last country in Northeast Asia to establish a diplomatic relationship with the United States. Soon after the ratification of the Korean–American Treaty (a.k.a. the Chemulpo Treaty) in 1882, which permitted Koreans to reside and work in all parts of the United States, a team of Korean diplomatic envoys visited the United States on a goodwill mission. In 1888, after the first Korean legation was established in Washington, D.C., a small number of Korean students, political exiles, ginseng merchants and migrant laborers began to arrive in America (Hurh & Kim, 1984: 39). However, it was not until a few years later that significantly more Koreans began to emigrate. As we will see, most Korean immigrants arrived in the United States in three major waves described in the following sections.

Labor immigration to Hawaii

Beginning in 1902, the Korean government established an immigration office in Seoul for recruiting Koreans to be employed in prospering sugar plantations in Hawaii. The sugar plantation owners in Hawaii turned to Koreans as a possible source of labor after the passage of the Chinese Exclusion Act of 1882, which prevented Chinese laborers from being employed in the plantations. More than 7,000 Koreans, most of them men, came to Hawaii looking for relief from economic hardship in Korea (Jo, 1999). Most of these early immigrants were laborers, ex-soldiers, students and political refugees, fleeing exploitation by the Korean government and increasing control by the Japanese, who eventually annexed Korea in 1910. They labored long hours under harsh conditions on sugar plantations or as cooks, janitors and launderers at subsistence wages. Unlike the more recent Korean immigrants who came to America to settle down indefinitely, the early immigrants had strong emotional ties to their homeland and intended to return to Korea as soon as they were financially able to do so.

In 1907, following the Gentlemen's Agreement between the US and the Japanese government, which essentially stopped Japanese and Korean immigration to the US, Koreans were no longer admitted to the US. However, Korean "picture brides" who contracted marriage to Korean immigrants on the basis of exchanges of photographs and correspondences, were continually admitted to the United States. Between 1910 and 1924, more than 1,000 Korean "picture brides" were admitted – most of them to join their spouses in Hawaii. However, from 1924 to the end of the Second World War when Korea was liberated from Japanese occupation, virtually no Koreans immigrated to the US, with the exception of several hundred students who eventually returned to Korea after completing their studies.

Post-Korean War immigration

The post-Korean War immigrants who arrived in the United States between 1951 and 1964 (a total of about 15,000) are the most heterogeneous but least studied group among Koreans in America (Jo, 1999). This immigrant group was composed of three categories: Korean wives of American servicemen stationed in Korea and war orphans, who together formed the majority of the group (77%), and professional workers (Hurh & Kim, 1984). The post- Korean War immigrants were markedly different from the early immigrants in that whereas the earlier labor immigrants to Hawaii were mostly male (ratio of 10 males to 1 female), there were more females in the second wave (ratio of 3.5 females to 1 male). Korean wives of US servicemen and a higher proportion of girls being adopted by American families contributed to this imbalance. The war brides of American GIs faced a range of problems associated with adapting to life in the United States and these are discussed at length in a number of studies (e.g. Kim, B.L. 1977; Lee, 1989). During this period, a small number of Korean students and doctors (about 2,000) whose education had been interrupted by the war came to study in US colleges and universities. Many of them returned to Korea to contribute to economic planning, scientific and technological research and development and educational planning which were desperately needed to rebuild a country devastated by war (B.L. Kim, 1988: 254).

Full-scale family immigration

The large-scale movement of Korean immigrants began only after passage of the US Immigration and Naturalization Act of 1965, which abolished the national origins quota system.[6] While this new legislation has had a dramatic impact on the volume and composition of Asian immigration to the United States in general, the increase in the number of Korean immigrants since 1965 has been especially remarkable. While a sizable number of Korean women entered the United States as wives of US citizens after the Second World War, the total number of immigrants who arrived in the 1950s was only 6,231. In the 1960s, however, the number increased five-fold to 34,526 and in the 1970s, it increased again by nearly 800% – to 267,638 (Mangiafico, 1988: 80). These new immigrants from Korea were characteristically very different from the older immigrants. Unlike the older immigrants, who were mostly illiterate, poor and low-skilled laborers, a majority of the new immigrants were educated, college-trained profes-sionals from the urban middle class of Korean society. They also came to the US as families, consisting of at least a husband, wife and one or more chil-dren (Jo, 1999).

Several factors have influenced the spectacular increases in the number of Korean immigrants in the third wave aside from the favorable changes in US immigration law. First, the Korean government relaxed its emigration policies. Following the founding of the Republic of Korea in 1948, emigra-tion was discouraged based on the reasoning that the nation required its population for economic development and defense against the communist north. This policy continued with minor changes until 1962, when emigra-tion policies began to be loosened due mainly to the government's attempt to control a huge increase in population after the Korean War (Mangiafico, 1988: 81). In addition, a military dictatorship, which was at the center of Korea's politics for nearly three decades (1961–1987), drove many Koreans to flee the country for economic and political freedom. The military govern-ment implemented a series of export-oriented economic policies that gave preferential treatment to large business conglomerates and placed small businesses at a distinct disadvantage. Furthermore, constitutional revisions under the military government recognized unprecedented executive powers and made it a crime to criticize the government, punishable by seven years to life in prison.

In the midst of such unfavorable economic and political circumstances at home, many Koreans saw the United States as a land of opportunity and freedom. In addition to the availability of better economic opportunities in America, many Koreans were drawn by the possibility of educating their children in the United States. Jo (1999) states that Korean professionals, such as college professors, researchers, medical doctors and engineers, came to America with the intention of studying at American universities and then returning to Korea. However, many remained in the US and brought their families to America, upon learning that their children could be educated at prestigious American universities for less expense than they could at top Korean universities. As I will argue later in this chapter and in Chapter 6, understanding the characteristics of Koreans' ambition for education is a requirement in a study of the language behavior of Korean American children.

I turn next to the social and demographic characteristics of Koreans in the US, focusing mainly on the latest and largest wave of Korean immigrants who arrived since the passage of the Immigration and Naturalization Act of 1965.

Social and Demographic Characteristics of Korean Americans

Nativity, sex, and age distribution

Of the Korean Americans enumerated in the 1990 Census, a vast majority (77%) was foreign-born, reflecting the relatively recent arrival of the group and the small population base of American-born Koreans. Over half of the nearly 600,000 foreign-born Koreans reported in the 1990 Census arrived in the US between 1980 and 1990, reflecting the enormous impact that the Immigration and Naturalization Act of 1965 had on Korean immigration. Of those who entered the US prior to 1980, 84% came between 1970 and 1980 (Mangiafico, 1988: 90). The 1990 Census revealed that there are more female Koreans (56%) than male Koreans (44%) living in the US, a marked contrast to the situation among the labor immigrants to Hawaii. Over the last four decades, the sex ratio of Korean Americans has favored females, partly due to a higher proportion of young Korean female children being adopted by American parents and the large number of inter-racial marriages of Korean women to US servicemen in Korea. While a trend toward a more balanced sex ratio is evident among the most recent immigrants, the effect of the past imbalance continues to be reflected in the present figures.

Koreans in the United States have a very young profile with a median age of 27 years for men and 29 years for women. While the working age group (20–64 years of age) comprises the largest proportion of the Korean population in the US, persons over 65 years of age are vastly under-represented when compared to the rest of the US population in the same age bracket.

Geographic distribution

As with most immigrants in general, Koreans prefer to reside in large urban settings, for a number of reasons. Since most of them came from urban areas, their skills can best be employed in an urban environment. In addition, an urban residence provides proximity to others of the same race or ethnic group who can provide considerable material and psychological support during the initial period of adjustment to life in the new country. Koreans are widely dispersed among all regions of the United States. According to the 2000 US Census, California maintains the largest Korean American population (see Table 2.1). The second largest group of Korean Americans lives in New York and New Jersey. Korean Americans constitute about 11% of the Asian American population in the US. In general, Korean immigrants tend to settle where other Koreans already reside – a normal pattern found in other ethnic groups. As can be seen in Table 2.1, the greatest increases in Korean population from 1990 to 2000 were seen in Georgia, New Jersey, Washington and Virginia.

Table 2.1 Top ten US destinations for Korean immigrants

State	Number of Koreans in the USA	As a percentage of total no. Koreans in the USA %	Percentage increase from 1990 Census
California	345,882	32	33
New York	119,846	11	25
New Jersey	65,349	6	70
Illinois	51,453	5	24
Washington	46,880	4	58
Texas	45,571	4	43
Virginia	45,279	4	50
Maryland	39,155	4	29
Pennsylvania	31,612	3	18
Georgia	28,745	3	88

Source: US Bureau of the Census, 2000 Census of the Population, Supplementary Reports (Washington, D.C.: Government Printing Office).

Educational attainment and occupation

Koreans in America are generally well educated. This is because the majority of the new immigrants who have arrived since the passage of the Immigration and Naturalization Act were educated, college-trained professionals from the urban middle class of Korean society. According to the 1990 Census, 55% of Korean Americans 25 years of age or over have had some college education and 80% have had at least a high school education: this compares with 45% and 75% respectively of all US citizens in the same age category. Despite their relatively high levels of education however, many Korean-born immigrants experience a great deal of difficulty finding jobs to match their education and professional training. This problem stems largely from their weak command of the English language, which is a significant source of frustration for Koreans. Upon their arrival in America, many Korean-trained professionals learn that they cannot readily secure professional employment due to their inability to communicate effectively in English. For example, in 1973, only a third of Korean-educated nurses in Los Angeles held state licenses, while 600 Korean-trained physicians in Southern California could not practice medicine because they could not obtain American licenses (Jo, 1999: 54). This is indeed a painful lesson for well-educated Koreans who must now settle for lower status, non-professional employment.

It is perhaps no wonder then that a high proportion of Koreans are concentrated in self-owned small businesses, which do not require high levels of English proficiency (or large start-up capital). For example, 32% of Korean households in the United States reported that they were engaged in small businesses and an additional 28% said they were thinking of opening a business (Mangiafico, 1988). In New York City, fully three-quarters of the Korean Americans are involved in small businesses – they own 1,400 produce stores (85% of all such stores in the area), 3,500 groceries, 2,000 dry cleaners, 800 seafood stores and 1,300 nail salons in the New York region (Goldberg, 1995). In the Chicago area, Korean businesses are also concentrated in the retail and service sectors (Kim & Hurh, 1985). While fruit and vegetable stands, grocery stores, service stations, and liquor stores are some of the favorite retail choices, accounting, real estate, building maintenance and repair services are the most popular service activities. Many of these businesses are owned and operated by Korean immigrants with excellent education and professional backgrounds but whose difficulty with English has driven them to non-professional work.

Korean businesses in large metropolitan areas often serve a clientele that has been neglected or abandoned by US businessmen: African Americans, Chicanos and Puerto Ricans (I. Kim, 1981; Hurh & Kim, 1984; Goldberg, 1995; Koehl, 1990). Korean merchants have come to play a middleman minority role, just as the earlier immigrants –Jewish, Italian, Greek, and Chinese Americans – had done in previous decades in low-income neighborhoods (Hurh, 1998). It is remarkable that most of these businesses are successful, given that the majority of the new Korean business owners had started their enterprises within three years of arrival in the United States and had had no previous business experience in Korea (Kim & Hurh, 1985). This success is largely attributed to Koreans' willingness to work hard and use ethnic financial resources and labor provided by family members. However, the success of Korean businesses in areas mainly populated by

African Americans has been a source of inter-group conflicts, resulting in organized boycotts by African Americans of Korean American stores and mass riots involving looting and arson of Korean businesses, such as that which occured in South Central Los Angeles in 1992 (for more on this, see Hurh, 1998; Min, 1996).

Education as a motive for immigration

As mentioned briefly before, one of the most important motivations for Koreans to immigrate to the United States is to seek better educational opportunities for their children (Hurh, 1998; Jo, 1999). To many Koreans, education represents the road to high social status and economic prosperity. Hurh (1998: 94) notes that Koreans' passion for education originates from the Confucian emphasis on learning as the best way to attain the wisdom and virtue needed by the ruling class in China:

> as early as 201 BC, China instituted a state examination system to select prominent Confucian scholars for high government posts. The Chinese examination system was adopted in Korea in AD 788; it provided men of intellectual ability with the most obvious route to political and financial success until the end of the Yi dynasty in 1905. This historical legacy of attaining social mobility through education is deeply rooted in Korean consciousness.

Therefore, providing children with the best possible education is most Korean parents' chief concern.

There are several factors that influence Koreans' search for better educational opportunities overseas. First, more and more Koreans are dissatisfied with the Korean educational system that emphasizes rote learning and memorization. There is little room for instructional flexibility and creative thinking in a rigid national curriculum, and more and more people believe that children need to be taught critical thinking and problem-solving skills, which are significantly lacking in the current system but are the hallmarks of western (e.g. American) education. Second, there are only a few universities in Korea that are recognized socially and competition to secure admission into one of these top universities is extreme. Many Korean children plug away 18-hour days and stay after school in cram schools until 10 or 11 at night before coming home, just to wake up at 5 or 6 the next morning to go to school again. A tremendous amount of pressure is placed on students to excel in school, which creates all sorts of physical, psychological and emotional stress in children. All of this has motivated some Koreans to look to educate their children outside of Korea, as one father describes:

My child failed his college entrance examination to enter one of the three best universities in Korea. My son was not much interested in entering one of the second- or third-rated universities in Korea as he knows he is not going to 'make it' after graduating from one of these universities because they are not the 'right' kind of universities. When I learned that my son could enter a very good university in the US with his high school grades, my wife and I decided to immigrate to the United States with him. My son enrolled in one of the top prestigious state universities, and we are very happy with his studies and with his university. Unlike Korea, there are so many excellent public and private universities from which a student can choose if she or he has very good grades. Now the problem is my wife and I have to look for something to do. Boredom is killing us. (Quoted in Jo, 1999: 36).

While the father quoted here probably had sufficient savings to quit his job in Korea and immigrate to the US with his family, many others are left without such choice. In fact, many fathers in Korea stay behind to work so that they can send money to cover the education and living expenses of their children who are enrolled in schools overseas and their mothers who must look after them. These stay-behind fathers, dubbed 'temporary bachelors' are so numerous in Korea today that they have formed various support organizations to exchange information about their children's foreign education (Moon, 2001). These fathers and mothers no doubt make immense physical and financial sacrifices for the children's education and family relations are necessarily strained as a result of long periods of separation. It is not clear what the long-term consequences of such separation might be for the tens of thousands of Korean families who have chosen this route to educate their children.

Koreans in America have the same kind of passion for education. For Korean Americans, talking about their children's educational and career success seems to be a way of making up for their lowered social status as shopkeepers and blue-collar workers in America (Jo, 1999). For example, second-generation Korean Americans often tell astonishing stories of their parents' obsession with the Ivy League. First-generation Korean immigrants know much about admission requirements at Ivy League and other prestigious institutions. In fact, it is often said jokingly that Korean parents are infected with the 'Ivy League disease' (Jo, 1999). Marie Lee, one Brown University-educated fiction writer (as cited in Goldberg, 1995), says that her father wrote away for Harvard University applications on the days each of his three children were born. A recent report indicated that Koreans made up 5% of the class of 1993 and 50% of total Asian enrollment at

Harvard Law School (*CrossCurrents*, 1996: 12). Similar numbers are reported at other top American colleges and universities (Goldberg, 1995). Given that Koreans make up less than 1% of the total US population, one cannot overestimate the Korean American commitment to education.

Like their counterparts in Korea, Korean parents in America pay a great deal of attention to their children's education. Korean American parents who live in or near large Korean American communities often send their children to after-school tutoring academies to prepare for admission to prestigious colleges and universities. According to Min (1995), about 20% of Korean junior and senior high school students in New York City take lessons after school, either in a private institution or with a private tutor. In Flushing, New York, about 20 tutoring academies (mostly owned and operated by Korean Americans) give English and math lessons to Korean American students (Min, 1995: 224). In terms of school choice, Korean American parents take school district rankings very seriously when deciding where to buy a house. As Min (1995: 224) notes,

> Most Korean immigrants with school-age children seem to decide where to live largely based on the academic quality of public schools in the neighborhood. Koreans' desire to buy houses in affluent suburban areas with good public schools is reflected in the 1990 census: Koreans, along with Indian Americans, show the highest rate of suburban residence among all ethnic groups.

Hurh (1998) notes that Korean American parents' passion for education and their willingness to sacrifice family resources for their children's education has enabled many Korean American children to excel in scholastic achievement, 'comparable to other Asian immigrant 'whiz kids' whose parents came from Hong Kong, India, and the Philippines in the 1970s'. However, parental pressure to get a good education and become successful in some professional career can often be excessive for children who resent being pushed beyond their capabilities to fulfill their parents' dreams. One second-generation Korean medical doctor describes:

> When I was growing up, my immigrant parents showed little interest in my social activities. The only thing they emphasized was: study, study, study – nothing else. Everything I had to do was their way not my way (Quoted in Jo, 1999: 110)

There are indeed various social and psychological costs to being 'a model minority' as a Korean American psychiatrist, David S. Rue, points out (cited in Hurh, 1998: 100):

While Asian-American 'Whiz Kids' have, no doubt, achieved an impressive level of academic success, their success has not come without a price. This price ranges from the frustration of a 16-year old Korean immigrant girl, whose classmates presume her to know all the answers to their homework, to a tragic death by suicide of a 17-year old Japanese American girl who died of 'pressure to succeed'.

How is Korean parents' emphasis on education related to language development in children? It is clear that, on the one hand, Korean American parents want their children to be academically successful and to receive college and advanced degrees from prestigious institutions. The parents are quite aware that their children must have strong English skills to achieve this sort of success in America. On the other hand, parents also want their children to retain full use of Korean as the language of social interaction in the Korean American home and community. Competence in both Korean and English is thus the most preferred attribute, which parents believe will enable their children to have equal access to both the world of the home and the larger society. However, the most common outcome for children of Korean immigrants in America is not bilingualism but monolingualism in English.

Although most Korean American children start out speaking Korean at home when they are young, most switch to English once they enter school. Since minority languages are not valued in schools, children do not see the need for learning and maintaining their native languages. In their attempt to be accepted by the English-speaking mainstream, immigrant children try hard to speak English like native speakers and may even try to forget the little Korean they already know, which labels them as 'different'. They start speaking English at home to their parents and siblings and respond in English to parents' utterances in Korean. Although some parents take great pains to prevent children from speaking English at home, most Korean parents think that English use among children is inevitable since they must be educated in English. In fact, as children switch to English, parents may also switch to it, at least when speaking with the children. This leads to a language shift in the family and there are fewer and fewer opportunities to speak the native language among family members. Without special efforts to preserve the mother tongue, English easily and overwhelmingly takes over as the main medium of communication among immigrant children. These issues will be explored in greater detail in Chapter 6.

The soaring popularity of English in Korea

At this point, I think a brief note about the current status of English in

Korea may help to provide an additional context to the perceived role of English in Korean American children's education and development. While English has traditionally been the most popular foreign language in Korea, there has been an intense renewed interest in learning the language in recent years, due partly to the Asian financial crisis of 1997, when hundreds of thousands of Koreans lost their jobs and the South Korean government turned to the International Monetary Fund for an economic bailout (Demick, 2002). Koreans realized how vulnerable they were to the international economy and how desperately they needed to know English in order to compete globally. More and more Koreans are taking English classes and an increasing number of young Korean children are being enrolled in English-speaking kindergartens. Demick (2002) states that there are now English-speaking preschools in Korea, where students, as young as 18 months old, are taught exclusively in English. A typical parent in Korea spends the equivalent of a month's salary on monthly tuition at English-language kindergartens and up to $50 an hour for tutors. This is possible since young parents in Korea today are more affluent than previous generations and normally have no more than two children. Demick estimates that between the after-school courses, flashcards, books, and videos, English instruction is a $3-billion-a-year industry in Korea – and that this figure does not include the expenses incurred by the tens of thousands of children sent abroad to attend schools.

Speaking English fluently without a Korean accent is deemed a highly desirable attribute in Korea, which some Koreans have taken rather extreme measures to achieve. In recent years, an increasing number of ordinary and otherwise healthy Korean children have undergone a tongue surgery known as frenectomy, which has been used for years to correct a condition popularly known as 'tongue-tie' (Demick, 2000). In this procedure, the thin band of tissue under the tongue – the frenulum – is cut, so as to enable the tongue to touch the roof of the mouth more easily. Demick reports that although this procedure used to be performed on children with excessively short tongues in the past, the popularity of this procedure has soared with the boom in English instruction. Korean parents believe that the supposedly longer and more flexible tongue resulting from the surgery can better produce English sounds that pose difficulties for Koreans such as the English 'r' in 'rice' which is often pronounced as 'lice'. Demick notes that most of the parents who bring their children in for surgery are themselves frustrated by an inability to learn English and want their children to have an easier time.

As extreme as it may be, the popularity of the tongue surgery reflects Korean parents' desire to find a quick-fix solution to overcoming difficulties with language acquisition. Speaking English with a foreign accent is perceived as a sign of imperfect acquisition, a muddled mixture of two phonologies. Popular belief is that bilingual speakers are expected to make a complete leap from one language to another without showing any trace of transference from one to another. However, as we have seen in Chapter 1, this belief is not supported by empirical linguistic evidence – bilingual speakers rarely have perfect competence in both languages in all domains and contexts.

Language use among Korean Americans

Just as fluent and unaccented English is sought with obsession in Korea, there is a prevailing belief among Koreans in the United States that fluency in English affords a certain status not available to those with little or imperfect fluency. Charles Ryu who immigrated to the US at the age of 17 comments:

> So among Koreans, language anxiety is very, very strong. If you speak good English, you tend to think you are better off than those that don't. And those who don't speak good English are often envious of those who can. So it is there; we don't speak about it (Quoted in Lee, 1991: 52).

Because Koreans find English so difficult to master, those who can speak fluent English are regarded with admiration and envy. They are regarded as having high status and this perception further contributes to language shift in the Korean American community. Korean parents are often reluctant to have their children be taught by teachers who speak English with a foreign accent. One director of a Montessori school with whom I spoke sometime ago informed me that the Korean parents specifically requested that their children not be placed in the class of one of the teachers who is Korean. The parents, seeing that this teacher spoke English with a Korean accent, did not want their children to learn the 'wrong' way of speaking English.

According to a survey conducted among Korean immigrants in the United States, English acquisition was ranked as the highest priority, but also as the most difficult task (B. L. Kim, 1988: 264). Since high proficiency in English is equated with prestige and economic and social success to many Korean immigrants, there is a strong desire among Korean Americans to learn English. However, most English language instructions that the immigrants received in Korea have been limited to book learning in high school and college, with very few opportunities to use and practice English in real life contexts. In America, working long hours in self-owned small businesses limits the opportunities for improving English by leaving immigrants with little time and energy to attend English classes. Given these facts, it is not surprising that first-generation immigrant communication among Korean Americans is almost exclusively in Korean. Several surveys have indicated that over 75% of spousal communication is in Korean (Kim *et al.*, 1980; Hurh & Kim, 1984). Kim *et al.* (1980) reported a low level of English proficiency among their respondents. Over one-third of the men and nearly half of the women indicated that their ability to speak English was 'poor' or 'not at all'. Only one-quarter of the men and one-fifth of the women rated their spoken English as 'good' or 'fluent'. This latter group of Koreans rated their reading and writing abilities to be even higher than their speaking abilities.

Consequences of lack of proficiency in English

The inability to speak English forces many Koreans to take low-paying jobs or perform menial tasks despite their high levels of education. This is face-threatening and damaging of one's self-image, which can create a great deal of stress and tension for the entire family. A first-generation immigrant describes how frustrating it is to not be able to speak English well:

> What good father am I? I can't go to see my daughter's teacher and discuss her academic progress. I have to ask my brother and children for help whenever I have to sign documents for buying and selling a house or a business, making a loan from a bank, and other government-related matters. I am getting tired of constantly asking someone for help. Also my entire family, including my wife, think that I am incapable of handling matters of significance. It is a constant embarrassment in front of my children and my wife when I can't understand exactly what a salesperson is saying in the department store, what a man is trying to say when I ask for directions, and what the mechanic is saying at the auto repair shop (Quoted in Jo, 1999: 118–119)

An immigrant woman who came to America with her parents when she was ten years old recalls a humiliating experience while interpreting for her father who spoke no English:

> I used to go with my father to translate for him at the store or bank. Once a woman asked if my father was my husband, even though I was only twelve years old. They couldn't differentiate. It was so humiliating for my father to have his daughter mistaken for his wife. What was heartless was to tell the child to translate threats and insults to their own parents, like 'Tell your father that if he does that next time, I'm going to sue him,' or 'Why can't he speak English? This is America'. I would just

translate the necessary facts. It's almost like people think they have a right to be inhuman to whoever can't speak English. (Quoted in Kim & Yu, 1996: 188)

As these testimonies show, parents' lack of English skills is a source of stress for both parents and their children. It is not uncommon for immigrant children to be asked to be language brokers in potentially sensitive situations (e.g. parent–teacher conferences) when there are no other persons who speak both the native language and English. While parents may be embarrassed that they must rely on their children for things that they should normally be able to do, children are also frustrated that their parents are so dependent on them for even very basic tasks.

Social and cultural adaptation of Korean Americans

As do other immigrant groups, Korean Americans feel a strong practical pressure to adopt various traits that are important for success in American society while at the same time to retain various cultural traits closely tied to their ethnic identity. In their survey, Kim *et al.* (1980) found that Korean American parents showed a strong desire for their children to retain Korean cultural traits, while at the same time wanting them to adopt seemingly opposite American cultural traits. For example, the overwhelming majority of the parents (99%) wanted their children to speak only Korean at home, and a large majority (over 90%) wanted their children to learn about Korean history and culture for their own self-identity, as well as to demonstrate such Korean cultural traits as 'respecting parents', 'being modest', and 'placing family needs and duties above individual interests'. However, these same parents wanted their children to adopt American cultural traits such as 'social assertiveness', 'openness and self-disclosure', and 'developing greater individuality'. An even more contradictory response was that 19% of the Chicago parents and 57% of the Los Angeles parents wanted their children to use only English at home. Kim *et al.* note that such incompatible responses reflect an American ideology and Korean parents' ambivalence about the acculturation of their children in America.

B. L. Kim (1988) and Hurh and Kim (1984) claim that this ambivalence, manifested in the contradictory responses in the studies, is fairly representative of the attitudes of the Korean American community in general. Hurh and Kim use the term 'adhesive adaptation' to characterize the acculturative process among the Koreans who are able to graft elements of the mainstream American way of life onto their own transplanted customs and manners. The relative ease with which Korean immigrants have maintained this 'adhesion' has been facilitated in part by subtle but widespread forms of social distancing from non-Korean groups that resist structural assimilation of racial minority groups.

The Social Networks of Korean Americans

The majority of Korean Americans maintain informal social relationships primarily with other Korean Americans: this is true regardless of their socioeconomic status, geographic location or the size or concentration of the local Korean population (B. L. Kim 1988: 265). Hurh and Kim's (1984) study of the Los Angeles Korean population indicated that high proportions of Koreans (75–90%) had close kin, neighbors and friends who were also Korean. More than half of the kin and a third of the neighbors were persons with whom they had daily contact: only a third had white friends and these were mostly people they had met through the workplace. Although a considerable number of Koreans work in racially mixed settings or, if in a small business, have regular commercial contact with Caucasian and African American, as well as Chinese and Latino American customers, the relationships thus established are confined to the workplace and remain largely secondary and formal. Instead, the Korean social network is drawn tightly at home, among family, friends, recreational colleagues and fellow church congregants.

Business associations such as the Korean American Grocers Association (KAGRO) and the Korean Dry Cleaning and Laundry Association serve major social functions among Korean Americans. Clan- or territory-based associations like those often found in Chinese or Japanese American communities as well as in Chinese communities in Britain (see Li, 1994) are rare (Kim & Yu, 1996). Instead, high school and college alumni associations and *kye* (rotating credit associations), a crucial source of capital for business and for children's college education often organized through high school and college alumni networks or church congregations, are key organizations in Korean immigrants' social and business lives (I. Kim 1981). In addition, senior citizens' clubs composed exclusively of Korean members is of particular importance to the Korean American community because elderly Korean Americans often cannot depend on the extended families from whom they would have received assistance (Kim, B.L., 1988). Aside from the social and business associations just mentioned, no other organization can match the Christian church in terms of size, influence and financial resources in the Korean American community (Kim & Yu, 1996). In the following, I discuss the role of the Korean American church in the lives of Korean immigrants.

Church involvement among Korean Americans

There are approximately 3,000 Korean Christian churches (most of them Protestant) in the United States today (Kim & Yu, 1996), which means that there is one Korean ethnic church for roughly 400 Korean Americans (Hurh, 1998). According to Kim's (1978) study of immigrant groups in the Chicago area, church participation by Korean immigrants was greater than that of any Asian American group except Filipinos. While the Chinese and the Japanese in Kim's study had Christian church affiliation rates of about 32% and 28% respectively, church affiliation among Koreans was 71%. Both Kim *et al.*'s (1980) and Hurh and Kim's (1984) studies have found that close to 80% of Korean Americans in Chicago and Los Angeles attend weekly services and over 25% of them hold non-paid staff positions in their churches. In New York City, more than 60% of the Koreans describe themselves as Christian but even a higher percentage of Koreans attends one of the region's 500 churches (Goldberg, 1995: 49). The large number of Korean immigrants who attend Korean churches in America is in contrast to the much smaller proportion of Christians in Korea (about a quarter of the population).

The unusually high rate of ethnic church participation among Koreans in America can be explained in part by the fact that about half of the new wave of Korean immigrants were already Christian prior to their emigration (Hurh, 1998: 109). Hurh notes that:

> Christianity in Korea has appealed mostly to urban classes attracted to Western ideas of progress and advanced science and technology. Often, to become a Christian in Korea meant to become Westernized or Americanized. This would explain why more Christians than non-Christians have immigrated to the United States, and why the majority of the former were urban dwellers.

In addition, the extensive church participation by Korean Americans can be explained by several unique functions that ethnic churches serve. Aside from satisfying the spiritual needs of its members through worship and fellowship, the Korean church also provides a place for its congregants to socialize with fellow émigrés and find peace of mind and relief from anxiety of living in a culture that is often hostile to immigrants. In addition, most Korean churches also serve as a central location for exchanging information and practical help which are often of vital importance in immigrant life; information about opportunities in employment, housing, schooling and vocational training is exchanged among the members. The clergy and fellow church members also provide assistance in translation, interpretation and filling out forms in English. Moreover, many Korean churches operate weekend Korean language schools for the children of their first-generation immigrant members.

Role of the church for second generation Korean Americans

As it does for first-generation Korean immigrants, the Korean ethnic church functions as a haven from 'white male standards in American society' for second-generation Korean Americans (Kim &Yu, 1996: XXI). Like their parents, second-generation Korean Americans display a high level of ethnic religious participation compared with other ethnic groups (Chong, 1998). While the language used in services and in fellowship in Korean American churches has traditionally been Korean, many churches now hold separate services in English for the mainly English-speaking second-generation Korean Americans. Chong (1998) argues that church participation among second-generation Korean Americans tends to be accompanied by a high degree of ethnic identity and consciousness. As an institutional vehicle for the cultural reproduction and socialization of the second generation, the Korean American church legitimizes and defends a set of core traditional Korean values and forms of social relationships, which constitute the main components of the second-generation identity. While second-generation Korean Americans consider their non-white race to be one of the most central traits of their identity, they also convey their ethnic identity by practicing certain traditional Korean cultural values. These values, apparent in their discourse about their Korean identity, consist of a set of core traditional Korean Confucian values – most significantly, filial piety, respect for parents, family-centeredness, and strong work ethic:

> My Korean values include respect for elders, emphasis on education. Another thing I love about Korean culture is its family-orientedness. I adore my parents. And I really like how children take care of their parents. ...There is a sense of comfort in being with other Koreans or Asians because there's an understanding in terms of background. For example, all Asian parents are strict. Korean Americans have an unspoken understanding that we've all been there, like experiences of prejudice (Quoted in Chong, 1998: 267)

Chong also argues that the Korean American church transmits and reinforces Korean culture among second-generation members through a variety of unwritten norms, rules and codes of conduct, which are transmitted and perpetuated at the level of everyday social interaction. For example, everyone in the church is expected to adhere strictly to the rule of respecting elders; the younger members are expected to display deference to older members even within the English-speaking second-generation congregation. In addition, there is a strict adherence to traditional gender roles – female members are expected to display traditional feminine behavior, such as behaving in a polite, subdued and non-aggressive manner. As important markers of ethnic and religious identity, these norms and rules of conduct are reproduced within the church among the second-generation through enormous pressures to conform. Chong states that the strong sense of ethnic identity observed among second generation church-goers reflects a form of defense against their perceived marginal status within American society as a non-white racial minority group. Thus, despite its role as a vehicle for the cultural interests of the first generation, the appeal of the Korean ethnic church for many second-generation members lies in its capacity to provide a refuge from this sense of margin-alization and along with it, positive social identity and group empowerment.

Current Immigration Trends

After about three decades of explosive growth, Korean immigration to the United States has seen a drastic decline in recent years. For example, the number of people in Korea who received immigration visas to the United States has fallen by more than half, from about 25,500 in 1990 to about 10,800 in 1994, according to the Bureau of Consular Affairs of the State Department. In comparison, the number of people returning to Korea has increased – between 5,000 and 6,500 people have returned to Korea in the same period, compared with about 800 in 1980 (Belluck, 1995). These are due mainly to the improved Korean economy and changes in US immigra-tions laws. Beginning in the latter part of the 1970s and continuing through the 1990s, South Koreans' standard of living has improved dramatically with rising per capita income every year (Jo, 1999). As a result, many professionals and economically established Koreans are no longer yearning to leave their country the way their predecessors did in the 1960s and the early part of the 1970s. While Koreans who immigrated 30 years ago had left a much poorer country with a military government, the more recent Korean immigrants have left a more democratic and economically more prosperous Korea.

In contrast to the improved economic conditions in Korea, many Korean small business owners in the US have been struggling to keep their busi-nesses open. For example, many New York City Korean American small businesses have experienced a downturn after about thirty years of growth. Estimates by the Korean American Small Business Service Center in

Flushing, New York, indicated that in 1994, 700 new Korean stores opened while 900 others closed (Goldberg, 1995). The struggling New York economy, coupled with the opening of neighborhood-busting megastores in various parts of the city, has forced hundreds of Korean-owned stores to shut each year. At the same time, the healthy Korean economy has drawn thousands of Koreans who raised families and built businesses in New York to return to Korea (Belluck, 1995). Belluck (1995) states that there are a number of cultural, social and economic reasons for moving back to Korea. For one, Koreans have never felt completely comfortable with the English language and the American culture. Others have become increasingly concerned about racial friction, violence and crime, while some want to contribute to the return of democracy in Korea, where the military government was toppled in 1987. But the most compelling reason is the healthier Korean economy.

If this trend of decreased immigration and increased return migration continues, the composition of the future Korean American community will change, affecting the maintenance of the Korean language in America. Since many of the children of Korean immigrants are well educated, they are likely to move into professional jobs, away from the traditional small businesses that tended to isolate their parents from properly participating in American society. With fewer new immigrants arriving from Korea and American-born Koreans losing proficiency in Korean at a rapid rate (or never acquiring it), a smaller proportion of the Korean American community is likely to be Korean-speaking.

In the next section, I provide a brief description of the structure of the Korean language.

Structure of the Korean Language

There has been much debate concerning the origin of the Korean language. Different hypotheses have been proposed to account for the structural similarity of Korean with other languages. One well-known hypothesis proposes a connection between Korean and the Altaic language family, which includes Turkic, Mongol and Manchu-Tungus branches (Crystal, 1987). The other hypothesis considers Korean as a language isolate with close links to another language isolate, Japanese. Korean and Japanese exhibit remarkable similarities in morphology, syntactic structures and other typological criteria (Martin, 1966; Kim, 1997). Like Japanese, Korean is an agglutinative language whereby infixes, prefixes and suffixes are added to the root to form new words. Example (2.1) below illustrates how tense is indicated through the addition of suffixes to the Korean root 'hata' (do):

(2.1) *ha.ta* – do(es)
hay.ss.ta – did
hay.wass.ta – have done
ha.ko.iss.ta – am doing (now)

Word order and postpositional markers

It is important to note the major typological differences between Korean and English. While English has a relatively strict word order of Subject–Verb–Object, Korean is a typologically Subject–Object–Verb language with relative freedom in word order (Martin, 1992; O'Grady, 1991; Kim, 1997). Such freedom in word order is possible in Korean because the grammatical roles of each constituent in a sentence are marked by postpositional case markers/particles, as shown in Example (2.2). Subjects in Korean take the nominative marker, *-ka* (following a vowel) or *-i* (following a consonant), while direct objects in Korean are followed by the accusative marker, *-(l)ul*. Indirect objects in Korean take a dative marker, *-hanthey*, or *-eykey*, while the topic marker, *-(n)un*, topicalizes nominative and accusative nouns by replacing their respective case markers, as shown in Example (2.3). In addition, a class of particles called 'delimiters' conveys information carried in other languages by articles, adverbs, prosodic elements or word order. Delimiters carry quantificational information and do not make the structural distinctions typically associated with case (O'Grady, 1991). In fact, as Examples (2.4) and (2.5) show, the same delimiter used with a dative particle can appear with a subject in lieu of the nominative marker, *-i*.

(2.2) *John-i*   *Sue-hanthey*   *kong-ul*   *cwu-ess-ta.*
John-NOM   Sue-DAT   ball-ACC   give-PAST-DECL
'John gave a ball to Sue.'

(2.3) *John-un*   *Sue-hanthey*   *kong-ul*   *cwu-n-ta.*
John-TOP   Sue-DAT   ball-ACC   give-PRES-DECL
'As for John, he gives a ball to Sue.'

(2.4) *John-i*   *Sue-hanthey-man*   *kong-ul*   *cwu-n-ta.*
John-NOM   Sue-DAT-DEL ('only') ball-ACC give-PRES-DECL
'John gives the ball only to Sue.'

(2.5) *John-man*   *Sue-hanthey*   *kong-ul*   *cwu-n-ta.*
John-DEL ('only')   Sue-DAT   ball-ACC give-PRES-DECL
'Only John gives the ball to Sue.'

Korean is classified as a null subject language. However, not only the subject of a sentence but also any or all of the nominal arguments of a predicate (i.e. verbs, adjectives and the copula), case markers attached to argument noun phrases and even the predicate itself may be dropped in Korean. A dropped argument or predicate is presumably 'old information' that the speaker thinks the listener will be able to recover from the context. In colloquial speech, any of the three nouns in Example (2.2) can be omitted when it represents old information: Case particles can also be dropped though with different frequencies: accusative markers are dropped quite frequently and nominative markers less frequently.

Relationship to Chinese

Historically, Chinese has exerted a strong influence on both Korean and Japanese in terms of its vocabulary and writing system. However, Chinese belongs to the Sino-Tibetan language family and is structurally quite different from Korean and Japanese. The Chinese writing system (ideographic characters, called *hanmwun* in Korean, *kanji* in Japanese) was first introduced to Korea in the first century and to Japan in the fifth century. For many centuries, in the absence of a Korean writing system, the Chinese system was used for written communication and scholarly pursuits mainly among people from the upper class (Hurh, 1998). Chinese characters are, however, incompatible with the spoken Korean language, since they are not phonetic but rather pictorial: each sign or symbol stands for the meaning of a word but not the sound of a word in Korean.

With King Sejong's invention of a highly efficient Korean phonetic alphabet, *hankul (hangul)*, in 1446, writing became far more accessible to ordinary people. Each of the 25 letters in *hankul* represents a single consonant or vowel – not a syllable as in Japanese, or a concept as in Chinese. Today, in Korea, a selected number of Chinese characters are still used in conjunction with the *hankul* alphabet, since many Chinese words have become an integral part of the Korean vocabulary (Hurh, 1998). A similar development also occurred in Japan: *kana* (a phonetic syllabic system based on the elementary strokes of Chinese characters) was devised in the ninth century and both kana and kanji (Chinese characters) are used today in combination.

Honorifics in Korean

The Korean language has one of the most complex honorific systems in the world, which reflects the highly rigid and stratified Korean social structure with its associated codes of etiquette to guide interpersonal behavior (Jo, 2001). In order to use honorifics in Korean, it is necessary to make a decision about the social relationship between the speaker and the addressee, as well as the subject and context of the talk (Kim, 1997). The speaker then makes a host of lexical and grammatical choices depending on his/her decision. For example, if the subject of the talk occupies a higher status (by age, family relationship, or social status) the subject honorific morpheme –*si* is attached to the end of the verb root '*cwu-*' ('give') as in Example (2.6).

(2.6) *apeci-ka   na-hanthey kong-ul   cwu-si-ess-ta.*
       father-NOM I-DAT   ball-ACC   give-HON:PAST-DECL
       'Father gave (HON) me a ball.'

To increase the degree of deference, the honorific nominative marker -*kkeyse* may replace the nominative marker –*ka* in the previous example. Korean grammar also features non-subject honorification, which replaces the verb with a suppletive form if the referent of a non-subject has a higher social status than that of the subject. This is shown by the suppletive verb '*tuli*' (give) in example (7):

(2.7) *nay-ka apeci-kkey   kong-ul   tuli-ess-ta.*
       I-NOM father-HON:DAT ball-ACC   give:HON-PAST-DECL
       'I (humbly) gave a ball to father.'

To pay respect to the addressee, or when speaking in a formal situation, a suffix indicating politeness –*upni* is added, as illustrated in example (8).

(2.8) *apeci-kkeyse   o-si-ess-upni-kka?*
       father-NOM :HON   come-HON-PAST-FORMAL-INT
       'Did father come (HON)?'

Here, as in Example (2.6), the subject honorific morpheme '-*si*' is used since the subject 'father' is the target of the speaker's deference.

Students of Korean experience a great deal of difficulty in learning the honorific system, which is one of the most important sociolinguistic skills to master in Korean. For students who are accustomed to English as their main language, which is far less elaborate in terms of honorific expressions, learning how to use honorific endings properly according to the contexts and characteristics of conversation partners can be exceedingly difficult (Jo, 2001). Although there are some basic rules systemizing the various styles of honorific verb endings (e.g. relative ages of the speakers), conversational contexts and relationships between speakers complicate the 'appropriate' choice of honorifics. To illustrate this complexity, Jo (2001) presents an erroneous sentence produced by a heritage speaker of Korean in a Korean language class at an American university:

(2.9) **Hyeng*   *kkeyse*   *nun*   *wuyu*   *lul*   *tus-ipni-ta.*
       Elder brother NOM (HON) NOM milk   ACC drink:HON-
                                                              FORMAL-
                                                              DECL
       'Elder brother drinks milk.'

Although this student applies the honorific rules vigorously to talk about an older person (namely, elder brother), the instructor points out that his honorific usage is too formal and inappropriate. The instructor comments that the honorific nominative marker *'kkeyse'* and the honorific verb *'tusipnita'* are too formal and recommends that they be replaced with their non-honorific counterparts. Example (10) below shows the instructor's version:

(2.10) *Hyeng*   *un*   *wuyu*   *lul*   *mashi-pni-ta.*
       Elder brother   NOM   milk   ACC   drink-FORMAL-DECL
       'Elder brother drinks milk.'

In order to help this student understand the honorific hierarchy among family members, this instructor draws a chart, putting grandparents at the top, father and mother on the next level and self and older siblings on the same level and younger siblings below oneself. The fact that self and older siblings are placed on the same level obviously creates difficulties for students who have been told that age is a main factor in determining honorific use. What complicates the matter further is that although generation and age differences determine family hierarchy, honorific rules are flexibly applied depending on the context. For example, while Example (2.11) is an ideal honorific expression, requesting an older person to eat, the less honorific version in Example (2.12) is also used commonly by many people.

(2.11) *apenim*   *cinci*   *capswu-sey-yo.*
        Father   meal:HON   eat:HON-HON-IMP:HON
        'Father, please eat.'
(12)   *apeci*   *siksa*   *ha-sey-yo.*
        Father   meal   do-HON-IMP:HON
        'Father, please eat.'

In sum, the intricate honorific system in Korean makes the language especially difficult to speak correctly, which poses problems for those who are trying to learn it. On the one hand, students who are not familiar with the subtle differences in the degree of formality and respect represented by the various lexical and grammatical choices, like the student in Example (2.9), may err on the side of being more cautious and sound overly formal and respectful. The flip side of this, of course, is that speakers who do not use proper forms of honorifics may come across to the addressee as being rude. For heritage learners of Korean, the use of honorifics poses special problems because Koreans are naturally less forgiving of language mistakes made by Korean Americans than they are of non-Koreans learning Korean. Because honorific use is such an integral part of the Korean language and culture, however, those who 'break the rules' are likely to be regarded as not genuinely Korean. This sort of sentiment is a major source of frustration and resentment among second-generation Korean Americans who are trying to learn the language well to be accepted by the Korean-speaking community. This issue will be discussed in further detail in Chapter 7.

Summary

In this chapter, I have reviewed the history of Korean immigration to the United States and described the demographic and social characteristics of Korean Americans. We have seen that in sharp contrast to the earlier Korean immigrants who were poor and uneducated, the later immigrants were highly educated middle-class citizens, most of whom had held white-collar occupations in Korea prior to their emigration but were unable to obtain jobs commensurate with their educational levels in the US due to their lack of English skills. This has led many Koreans to stress the impor-tance of acquiring English, which contributes to language shift in the Korean American family and community. I have also attempted to explain the sociolinguistic situation of Koreans in the US by paying special atten-tion to the social networks of Korean Americans. We have seen that the majority of Korean Americans are involved in social networks participated in primarily by other Korean Americans. The same holds true for many second-generation Korean Americans who, though English-speaking, expe-rience difficulty joining social networks participated by Anglo Americans due to their racial minority appearance. The Korean American Christian church plays a crucial role in providing a venue for the transmission and maintenance of certain ethnic values.

In sum, Korean Americans, as do other immigrant groups, feel a great deal of social and economic pressure to adopt various traits that are crucial for success in American society while, at the same time, wanting to main-tain their ethnic language and culture. English acquisition is the highest priority for many Korean immigrants but also the most difficult task. The vast structural differences in English and Korean are a great source of diffi-culty and as most immigrants' former learning of English was limited to translation-based text-driven instruction, many Koreans experience difficulty in spoken English. Parents are frustrated with their own inability to speak English without an accent and are determined to see their children gain full proficiency in English. This intense desire to speak native-like English, coupled with an unmatched passion for education has accelerated the Americanization of second-generation Korean immigrant children. Without systematic support for Korean maintenance, many of these children have, in turn, become fantastically monolingual in English, unable to communicate even at basic levels with their mostly Korean-speaking parents. Parents often feel powerless to reverse the natural course of Americanization or 'Englishization' (Zentella, 1997: 266) of their children, who, in turn, feel pulled by the demands of their two very different worlds.

Chapter 3

Methods

In this chapter, I describe the four separate sources of data that serve as a basis for the discussion found in the next three chapters:

(1) spontaneous speech of 12 Korean American first-grade children in their mainstream classroom in a New York City public school;

(2) experimental language data elicited from the twelve Korean American children;

(3) survey data obtained from 251 Korean American parents with school-age children; and

(4) follow-up interviews with selected survey respondents and their children.

First, I provide an account of my access into the school where I collected the language data and offer a description of the children's background, the teachers and the school. I describe my role as a participant observer in the classroom and the situations in which the audio-recordings of the children's bilingual speech were made. I then describe the experimental procedure aimed at obtaining insight into the children's grammatical development in Korean and English.

Spontaneous Speech Data

Access to the school

The spontaneous language data were collected in May and June of 1995 in a first-grade mainstream classroom in a public elementary school in New York City, which I will call Hillside Elementary.[7] The class consisted of 27 first-graders, 12 of whom were Korean. This provided me with an exceptional opportunity for data collection and observation of Korean children interacting with both Korean and non-Korean classmates. Since all 12 Korean students were present in one classroom for at least five hours a day for five days a week, I was able to collect a large amount of language data in a relatively short period of time without having to search out individual children scattered in different classrooms. I had a particularly easy access into the setting because the homeroom teacher (Mrs Kim) and I have been friends for many years. Mrs Kim had been teaching this first-grade class since September 1994 and possessed an excellent knowledge of each of her students' academic progress and backgrounds and maintained close contact with the parents. Making use of such existing personal networks based on friendship proved to be extremely useful for this type of sociolinguistic research (see also Hammersley & Atkinson, 1995). I was given permission by the school principal to collect data in Mrs Kim's classroom and record children's speech with their parents' written consent, which was readily secured.

Programs for language minority children at Hillside Elementary

The high proportion of recent immigrant population in this part of New York City is reflected in the composition of Mrs Kim's first grade classroom. Aside from the 12 Korean students, this class consisted of five Chinese, one Afghan, one Russian, and six Hispanic students who came from homes that spoke a language other than English. Only two out of the 27 students were native speakers of English. Overall, this school has a high proportion of immigrant students – about 700 of the 970 students enrolled in the school speak English as a second language. More than half of the student population at this school is of an Asian descent. The relatively low income level of the parents is reflected in the large percentage of student population (about 70%) that is eligible for free and reduced meals. In addition, with a continuous stream of new immigrants arriving in the neighborhood, and with limited resources, the school has difficulty keeping its classes small. For example, Mrs Kim's class has 27 students, which is doubtless high for one teacher to manage but is within the school norm.

Hillside Elementary has Korean, Chinese, and Spanish bilingual programs. There are two Korean–English bilingual teachers, each in charge of kindergarten–3rd grade, and 4th grade–6th grade bilingual classes. In the beginning of each school year, the school administers English proficiency tests to all students whose native language is not English. Students who do not achieve a passing score are placed in a daily pull-out ESL class. There are two levels of ESL classes – regular and low level – both of which are taught by a monolingual English-speaking teacher. Students whose native language is one of Korean, Chinese or Spanish also attend a daily pull-out bilingual class in addition to the ESL class. Korean, Chinese, and Spanish speaking students therefore receive two periods of pull-out instruction per day whereas other language minority students receive one daily pull-out ESL instruction.

The bilingual education model adopted at Hillside Elementary is a weak variation of a transitional early-exit model (see Skutnabb-Kangas, 2000).

Unlike typical transitional bilingual education programs, in which language minority students are taught more or less in both languages for the entire school day, this school has a pull-out bilingual education model, where students are taken out of their mainstream classrooms one period per day for bilingual instruction. This type of bilingual instruction simply acts as extra remedial assistance to students' development of English in addition to ESL instruction (which is all in English) and has no goal of developing and maintaining students' first languages. Students are tested annually on their skills in English (but not in their native languages) and upon achieving a passing score, are moved out of both ESL and bilingual classes. The bilingual classes are thus seen to provide additional help for students' English development and are dropped as soon as students are deemed able to function in English-only classrooms without mother-tongue assistance. The goal of such programs clearly is assimilation and integration of the minority-language speakers into the English-speaking mainstream, not maintenance of their native languages.

The Korean Children

Twelve Korean children in Mrs Kim's first-grade classroom – six male and six female – served as subjects for the language data. All 12 children had Korean as their native language. Each child's name, sex, age at the beginning of the data collection period, as well as ESL and bilingual education class status are listed in Table 3.1. Besides Matthew, Joshua, Abel and Kyung who were born in the US and Gina who was born in Argentina, all the other children were born in Korea and had subsequently moved to the US with their families. Kwon's family had moved to Mexico soon after his birth and then came to the US when he was four years old. Except for David, whose first contact with English was in Mrs Kim's first-grade class, all the other 11 children had attended English-speaking kindergarten in the US before coming into this first-grade class.

Ten of the 12 Korean children were enrolled in a daily pull-out Korean–English bilingual class and a separate pull-out ESL class. Matthew and Kyung had passed the school board's English proficiency test at the beginning of the school year and, thus, were exempt from these two classes. Two levels of ESL pull-out classes (i.e. beginner and intermediate) taught by a monolingual English-speaking teacher served kindergarten through third-grade English language learners at this school. Except for David who was enrolled in the beginner level class, the other nine Korean children attended the intermediate ESL class. However, all ten children went to the same Korean–English bilingual class one period per day. When the English proficiency test was administered again in April 1995, Grace, Kathy, Gina, and So Hee also achieved passing scores and were to be mainstreamed starting with the second grade.

Table 3.1 *Korean subjects*

Name	Sex	Age	ESL/Bilingual
David	M	7:2	Yes
Kwon	M	7:0	Yes
Matthew	M	7:0	No
Jae	M	6:9	Yes
Joshua	M	6:7	Yes
Abel	M	6:6	Yes
So Hee	F	7:4	Yes
Kathy	F	7:0	Yes
Gina	F	6:11	Yes
Yooni	F	6:9	Yes
Kyung	F	6:7	No
Grace	F	6:7	Yes

The Teacher

Mrs Kim, the homeroom teacher, immigrated to the United States at the age of seven with her family from Korea. After that, she received her elementary, secondary and college education in the US. While her ability in Korean has not progressed much since moving to America, Mrs Kim can nevertheless carry on a simple conversation in Korean and speaks Korean with the Korean parents of her students. There is no trace of a Korean accent in her English but some of her Korean students attempted to speak to her in Korean at the beginning of the school year. Mrs Kim reported having specifically instructed her Korean students not to speak to her in Korean out of consideration for the non-Korean students in her class. The fact that 10 of her 12 Korean students had the opportunity to speak Korean in the daily pull-out Korean–English bilingual class also led her to insist on English as the main language in her classroom. However, although she did not allow her Korean students to address her in Korean, Mrs Kim did not prevent them from speaking Korean among themselves. Mrs Kim also spoke some Spanish, of which she made very good use when meeting with some of the Spanish-speaking parents. Mrs Kim, as a Korean American, is definitely in the minority in the teaching faculty at Hillside Elementary – over 85% of the teachers there are white.

Participant observation as a teacher's aide

I adopted the role of a classroom assistant, participating in the daily routines of the class. This allowed me to collect a tape-recorded corpus of spontaneous speech and to observe children's language choice and language-mixing patterns without considerably imposing my presence as a researcher. Furthermore, because Mrs Kim had supervised student teachers during the academic year, the children were accustomed to having adults other than their teacher in the classroom, making my presence in the classroom natural. I assisted Mrs Kim with whatever task she need assistance – attending to individual student's work, escorting students to and from the cafeteria and gym, cleaning after the day is over and taking charge of the class in cases of emergency. Whenever possible, detailed notes of class activities, events and children's language use were taken throughout the course of the day. These notes proved to be useful in understanding the children's language use when used in conjunction with the spontaneous language data.

Unlike the homeroom teacher who spoke only English and instructed her Korean students to speak English to her, I spoke both English and Korean when addressing the Korean children – a behavior which appeared to be acceptable to both students and the teacher. This was done to see how the children would respond to utterances made in both languages by an adult bilingual speaker. Since the default language of the classroom is English, my use of both languages was likely to create additional occasions for these bilingual children to codeswitch. However, although I tried hard to elicit Korean speech by speaking Korean to the Korean children, I generally ended up speaking far more English than Korean – overall, I think I spoke about 80% of the time in English and about 20% of the time in Korean. In this sense, I, too, was probably adjusting to the monolingual norms of this mainstream classroom and speaking Korean only when the situation called for it. The main goal in the speech elicitation process was to gain insight into the structure of everyday spoken language of the bilingual children engaged in various classroom-related activities. Such ethnographically-sensitive, modified participant observation procedures – where the researcher produces relevant, socially situated talk as a participant in the classroom as well as observing the class – allow observation of classroom with minimum observer effect (Milroy & Gordon, [2003]; see also Moffatt & Milroy [1992]; Lin [1988, 1990] for reports of similar studies of different groups of bilingual children at school).

Recording of the speech data

Each child being recorded wore a small lightweight wireless radio microphone. Sound signals were transmitted to the radio receiver connected to a cassette-recorder placed inconspicuously in a box in the back corner of the classroom. The lightweight wireless transmitter–receiver system recorded speech from any part of the classroom while allowing children to move around freely as they were accustomed to. Based upon Mrs Kim's evaluations of students' language proficiency, the 12 Korean students were organized as six pairs such that members of each pair showed comparable proficiency in both English and Korean, as shown in Table 3.2. This was done to prevent significant mismatch in bilingual proficiency between students and to obtain the largest possible amount of conversational data.

Table 3.2 The subject sample showing pairing arrangements

Pair	
1	Kyung and Matthew
2	Yooni and Grace
3	Kathy and Gina
4	Kwon and Joshua
5	Abel and Jae
6	David and So Hee

Audio recordings were made in three situations:

(1) *storytelling*, telling to the partner a spontaneously created story or some other account based upon an activity in class.
(2) *math*, involved counting in some form, such as in buying and selling toy goods in an imaginary store, sorting and counting different plastic shapes, or measuring how far a snail travels in a given amount of time; and
(3) *play*, occurred as part of the 'Learning Center' activity, in which children are free to play educational games with one another (e.g. various board games, wooden blocks, and jigsaw puzzles).

The recordings for each activity type lasted between 20 and 75 minutes per pair, yielding a total of approximately 10 hours of recorded speech. For the analysis of codeswitching found in Chapter 4, all codeswitch sites as well as several utterances both before and after the codeswitches were transcribed along with relevant contextual and situational information. Utterances in English were put in caps while utterances in Korean were lowercased, italicized and followed by both a morpheme-by-morpheme translation and a normal translation (for sample transcriptions, see Chapter 4).

Bilingual Acquisition: Grammatical Morpheme Data

In addition to the children's codeswitching behavior, I examined one specific aspect of the children's bilingual acquisition with respect to their acquisition of English grammatical morphemes (an introduction to morpheme acquisition studies is found in Chapter 1). The nature and extent of bilingual children's first- and second-language acquisition are of great interest to parents, educators and researchers. In this book, I present a description of one feature of the language learning of the Korean American children. Following Brown's (1973) finding that there is a common, invariant sequence of acquisition for at least 14 bound morphemes by children acquiring English as their native language, researchers have examined the developmental sequences followed by children acquiring English as a second language. These studies attempt to determine whether the sequence found by Brown is also found in children acquiring English as a second language and whether children of different first-language backgrounds acquire grammatical morphemes in the same sequence. I address this question by comparing the Korean American children's order of acquisition of ten English grammatical morphemes (a detailed description to follow) to that of monolingual English-speaking children and several groups of English-language learners with different first-language backgrounds (Chinese, Spanish, and Japanese, and Korean). The main goal of this analysis is to investigate crosslinguistic differences in language acquisition patterns with specific reference to the English acquired by the Korean American children.

The morpheme study used the children's spontaneous speech (only the English portion) described earlier. I have adapted Dulay and Burt's (1974) procedures for scoring morphemes (see Chapter 1 for background information on this study). Table 3.3 shows the 10 English grammatical morphemes investigated.

Table 3.3. The 10 English grammatical morphemes examined in the experimental study

Morphemes	Structures	Examples
Pronoun case	Pro–(Aux)–(Neg)–V–(Pro)	*She* doesn't like *him*.
Article	(Prep)–Det–(Adj)–NP	*The* girl wanted a pumpkin.
Copula	NP–(*be*)—Adj or NP	It'*s* my turn.
Progressive	NP or Pro–(be)–V+ing	They're clean*ing* up.
Plural	NP+pl	Circle*s*.
Auxiliary	NP or Pro–*be*–V–ing	They'*re* cleaning up.
Past regular	NP or Pro–V+pst–NP or Pro	She want*ed* a ball.
Past irregular	NP or Pro–V+pst–NP or Pro	I *knew* we got it.
Possessive	N+poss	*My* book; John'*s* book.
Third person	NP or Pro+sing–V–tns–(Adv)	The circle goe*s* here.

The analysis incorporates the notion of 'obligatory occasion' adapted from Brown's (1973) study, adopted also by Dulay and Burt (1974). Obligatory occasions are stretches of talk consisting of more than one morpheme where particular grammatical morphemes are required. For example, in the utterance 'She is eating', mature native speakers of English do not omit the morpheme -*ing*, which is obligatorily attached to any verb in English in the context 'BE   V _ #'. A child who is in the process of learning a second language will put on such obligatory occasions but may not furnish the required forms. They may be omitted altogether, as in 'he like hamburgers' or misformed, as in 'he eated his lunch' where the regular past form -*ed* is incorrectly supplied. Each obligatory occasion for a grammatical morpheme was treated as a 'test item' and scored as follows:

- no morpheme supplied   = 0 (She take it),
- misformed morpheme supplied   = 1 (She taked it),
- correct morpheme supplied   = 2 (She took it).

Details of items scored are as follows:

(1) *Pronoun case*: pronouns were scored for correct case-marking whenever they appeared, i.e. in subject position (i.e. *he, she, they, we, I*), in indirect or direct object position (i.e. *him, her, them, us, me*), and immediately following prepositions. *It* and *you* could not be scored for case as the form remains the same in all positions.

(2) *Article*: tokens of both *a* and *the* were combined under the general category 'article'.[8]

(3) *Copula*: singular and plural as well as present and past copula tokens were tallied together.

(4) *Progressive*: -ing was tallied when preceded by past or present forms of 'BE'. Gerunds were not included in the tally.

(5) *Plural*: only the so-called 'short plurals' were included, i.e. /s/ and /z/ allomorphs attached to nouns such as desk-*s* and circle-*s*.[9]

(6) *Auxiliary*: Present and past as well as singular and plural forms of *be* were combined under one category. This category excluded modals (e.g. *may, can, will*).

(7) *Past regular*: All allomorphs of the past regular (/t/, /d/, and /Id/) were included.

(8) *Past irregular*: these included only main verbs, such as *ate, stole, got,* and *fell*. In cases where a child offered 'eated,' past irregular was scored as a misformation.

(9) *Possessive*: possessive marker '*s* on nouns as well as possessive pronouns were tallied.

(10) *Third person singular*: these were scored whenever a singular noun phrase or pronoun appeared in subject position immediately followed by a main verb. *Does* and *has* used as main verbs were not included in the tally.

The group score for a particular morpheme is obtained by dividing the scores for each obligatory occasion of that morpheme (across all children) by the sum of all obligatory occasions (where each occasion is worth two points) for that morpheme across all children. To illustrate the scoring method, consider the following five utterances produced by three children and compute the group score for the past irregular.

		Raw Score	Occasion
Child 1:	He eated it.	1	2
	This man taked it away.	1	2
Child 2:	He bite it.	0	2
Child 3:	He stole it.	2	2
	The dog took it.	2	2
Total		6	10

Group Score = 6/10 X 100 = 60

The procedure then was to rank the ten grammatical morphemes according to decreasing group score. The Korean children's rank order of acquisition is compared in turn with the following: Brown's (1973) English monolingual subjects; Dulay and Burt's (1974) Chinese-speaking and Spanish-speaking subjects; Hakuta's (1976) Japanese learner of English;

and Pak's (1987) Korean learners of English in Texas. In Chapter 5, I discuss the results of a series of Spearman rank order correlation tests with reference to previous claims regarding second-language acquisition of grammatical morphemes.

Bilingual Acquisition: Experimental Data on Plural Marking

Of the ten English grammatical morphemes examined, the plural presented the greatest difficulty to the Korean American children (see Chapter 5 for the results of the morpheme study). The primary goal of the experimental study was to investigate the extent of acquisition of plural marking in Korean and English by the bilingual children as compared to same-age monolingual children of both languages.

Materials for the experimental study on plural marking

The experiment used 48 laminated flashcards with either photographs or colored drawings of common objects or animals to elicit children's responses. Each card illustrated either one or two of a given item and presentations were ordered so that a card with a single item preceded a card with two of the same items (e.g. card 1 illustrated one watch, card 2 two watches, card 3 one chair, card 4 two chairs, card 5 one sock, card 6 two socks, and so on). Two matched stacks, each with 24 cards (12 different items), were prepared as shown in Table 3.4. Stack 1 was presented with instruction in English and Stack 2 with instruction in Korean. Every item illustrated in Stack #1 corresponded to a semantically related item in Stack 2. Care was also taken to ensure that an established English borrowing in Stack 1 (e.g. camera) corresponded to such item in Stack 2 (e.g. TV) and a noun that is normally used in the plural in Stack #1 (e.g. sock) corresponded to such item in Stack 2 (e.g. shoe). In order to minimize the order effect, six students were randomly selected to receive Stack 1 before Stack 2, while the other six received the two stacks in the opposite order (see Table 3.5).

How number is expressed in English and in Korean

English expresses number in various ways. Number may modify the noun (e.g. 'two candies') or modify a representative counter (e.g. 'two pieces of candy') or used as a noun substitute (e.g. 'I want two [of them]'). Different languages show different degrees of flexibility in the number structures that they allow. Korean is fairly flexible but some of the possible constructions occur more frequently than others. Similar to the English

Table 3.4 Words tested in the experimental task

Stack 1	*Stack 2*
watch	clock
chair	table
sock	shoe
cat	dog
tree	flower
knife	spoon
car	airplane
apple	watermelon
block	ball
snake	bird
pencil	book
camera	TV

plural suffix //s//, a suffix, *-tul* marks plural in Korean. However, *-tul* is optional and is used relatively infrequently (Martin, 1992). Two classes of words modify the noun in Korean: numerals and classifiers. A classifier occurring after a numeral can be one of mainly two types: unit and measure. A unit classifier counts individual instances of a countable noun as in Examples (3.1) to (3.3).

(3.1)   *chayk han kwen*   book one [CLASS] 'one book'
(3.2)   *kay twu mali*   dog two [CLASS] 'two dogs',
(3.3)   *pay sey chek*   boat three [CLASS] 'three boats'.

In comparison, a measure classifier conveys the amount of a measurable noun as in Example (3.4), or of money as in (3.5).

(3.4)   *cha han can*   tea one [CLASS] 'one cup of tea',
(3.5)   *chen wen*   thousand [CLASS] 'a thousand wen'.

While some countable nouns in Korean require specific unit classifiers, many others lack specific classifiers and number is expressed by the numeral alone; in fact, the bare numeral without a classifier can be used to count any noun. While it is possible for some nouns to occur in constructions where a numeral is placed before the noun, as would be the case when a unit counter (e.g. *salam* [person] in *haksayng han salam* [one student]) is used as a free noun (e.g. *[salam] han salam* [one person]), the most common order in Korean is Noun–Num–(CLASS) (Martin, 1992). For example, while *thokki hana* [lit. rabbit one – 'a rabbit'] and *talk hana* – [lit. chicken one – 'a chicken'] are acceptable, **han thokki* –[one rabbit – 'a rabbit'] or **han talk* –[one chicken – 'a chicken'] are not.

Elicitation procedures for the experimental study on plural marking

The experiment consisted of two different tasks administered approximately two weeks apart. In the first task, each child sat individually with me and responded to what was being asked in an interview. In the second task, a more spontaneous type of language data was obtained by having two students in a pair administer the task to each other. Both parts of the experiment were audio-recorded.

Interview task

The first task (interview task) procedure was as follows. Two stacks of flashcards, one to be presented with an instruction in Korean and the other with an instruction in English (see Table 3.4) were separately placed facing down on the table in front of the child. I asked the child to pick up a card on the top of the designated stack, place it in front and state the name of the item (e.g. 'watch/a watch'). If the child did not mention the number (i.e. 'one'), I asked 'How many?' to which the child responded 'One'. I then rephrased the response by saying emphatically, 'ONE watch, right?'. The child agreed and then picked up the next card from the pile, placed it on top of the first card and stated 'two watch(es)'. Again, if the child did not mention the number (i.e. 'two'), I asked 'How many?' to which the child responded 'Two'. I then said 'Okay, so there are TWO – what?' to which the child either responded 'Watches' or 'Watch'. I then repeated the child's response by saying 'Can you say two watches?' In order to minimize the order effect, six children were randomly selected to receive Stack 1 with the English instruction first, while the remaining six received Stack 2 with the Korean instruction first (see Table 3.5). Two native speakers of English in this class performed the same task as a control group, with instructions for both stacks given in English.

Table 3.5 Order of testing for the experimental task on plural marking

Stack # 1 First	*Stack # 2 First*
Kyung	Abel
Jae	Kathy
Grace	Joshua
Gina	Kwon
David	Matthew
Yooni	So Hee

Game Task

The second task (game task) was administered two weeks later to investigate whether the children's use of the plural marker in the first task (interview setting) was consistent with their use in more spontaneous speech. Two Korean children in a pair (see Table 3.2) sat facing each other across a table. One child was given Stack 1 and the other Stack 2 and both children were instructed in English to play a game in which each child described items shown on the cards to his/her partner. I instructed the children not to show their cards to their partners until they finished describing them. I explained that they were to provide each other with descriptions of objects shown on the cards including size, shape, color and number so as to enable the partner to visualize it. What I expected to obtain from the game task were occasions for the plural morpheme embedded in spontaneous speech. Both stacks contained cards in the same order as in the interview task. After presenting the instructions, I left the area to ensure that the children spoke with each other. The results of the two experimental tasks are discussed in Chapter 5.

Survey Data

To supplement the findings from the children's language data, a survey was administered to Korean American parents with school-age children to gain further insight into the bilingual development and socialization patterns at home. First-generation immigrant Korean American parents of school-age children (between the ages of 4 and 18, in preschool through high school) were solicited through Korean American churches in four US cities.[10] The survey contained 53 questions in Korean intended to elicit information about various aspects of bilingualism and language shift and maintenance in Korean American families. The survey was based on reports of language use, attitudes, social and cultural practices and efforts to maintain Korean in various familial and institutional settings. The questionnaire elicited the following information: (a) demographic details; (b) parents' proficiency in Korean and English; (c) parents' and children's use of Korean and English in different domains; (d) parents' attitude toward the use of Korean and English in various situations; (e) literacy practices at home; and (f) parents' efforts and attitudes toward the development of bilingualism in their children. The survey can be found in Appendix 4.

Three of my extended family members, based in large Korean American churches in Chicago, Houston and New York, served as focal contacts and assisted in the distribution and collection of questionnaires in those cities. I was in charge of the distribution and collection of questionnaires in Baltimore. The completed questionnaires were either mailed to me in self-addressed stamped envelopes or returned to the focal contact persons, who then forwarded them to me. Out of the 411 originally distributed, 251 questionnaires (61%) were returned. This strong response rate for the survey may reflect the interest in children's bilingualism among Korean American parents.

Interview Data

To learn more about language attitude and language use among parents and children, 12 survey respondents were contacted for interviews. The 12 were selected on the basis of my existing relationships with them through church and other activities and consisted of parents of children of different ages. They were quite representative of the 251 survey respondents in terms of demographic backgrounds and bilingual proficiencies. Whenever possible, the respondents' children were also interviewed either separately or together with their parents. The interviews were semi-structured and guided by the following questions:

(1) In your opinion, how important is English (Korean) in your children's success in school and in American society?
(2) How important is it for you to have your children be proficient in Korean?
(3) What do you do to support your children's development in English (Korean)?
(4) Do your children know how to read and write in Korean? If so, how did they learn to read and write in Korean? How do their literacy skills measure up against their speaking and listening skills in Korean?
(5) What difficulties have you had in teaching English (Korean) to your children?
(6) What kind of support do you need to teach English (Korean) successfully to your children?

In addition to answers to these questions, interviewees were asked to provide any pertinent information they thought would be helpful. Each interview lasted between 30 minutes and two and a half hours and took place either in the homes of the respondents or on the phone. When invited to the respondents' homes, I made observations of informal family interactions and noted the types of literacy activities occurring in both languages. I noted who spoke what language to whom and when, the availability of printed materials in either language and TV programs that were watched. The results of the survey and the follow-up interviews are discussed in Chapter 6.

In the next three chapters, I take up the task of examining the empirical evidence related to the bilingualism of Korean immigrant children. The concluding chapter provides an overview of the specific issues considered in these three chapters and makes recommendations for bilingual and heritage-language education of Korean American and other language minority children.

Chapter 4

Codeswitching as a Communicative Resource

In this chapter, I look at ways in which the Korean American children use bilingual codeswitching to accomplish specific communicative goals. I have already noted in Chapter 1 that very few bilinguals keep their two languages completely separate. Quite contrary to the popular assumption that codeswitching is a haphazard blend of two languages, it conveys the speaker's intents, attitudes, emotions and preferences at any given moment to other participants in the conversation. In this chapter, I show evidence that children use codeswitching as a valuable communicative resource to structure their discourse.

In Chapter 3, I noted that the 12 Korean children share a common cultural and linguistic heritage. Being members of the Korean immigrant community in New York City, the children learned to speak Korean at home and were later exposed to English at school. However, the 12 children constitute anything but a homogeneous group, as each demonstrates uniquely different bilingual speech patterns. The children possess different proficiencies in Korean and English, hold different views about the value of bilingualism, as evidenced in their preference for speaking one or the other language in various settings and have different personalities and disposi-tions. While some children are more English-speaking, others are Korean-dominant. Some feel awkward about using Korean in the presence of non-Korean peers in the classroom but others purposefully use Korean as an in-group code with other Korean children. Some mix the two languages quite frequently and extensively, whereas others hardly ever switch between the two languages. However, as we shall see in this chapter, each child strategically chooses his/her languages to accomplish specific social and communicative purposes.

In the mainstream classroom where the speech data for this study were collected, English is the expected language and is indeed the most frequently chosen mode of communication among the Korean children. Codeswitching is found in only a small portion of the speech data and some

18	**Mrs Kim:**	OKAY NOW LOOK AT THE EYES/
19		LOOK AT THE EYES/
20		AND THEN LOOK AT THE MOUTH/
21	**Jae:**	EAT IT/

(Mrs Kim walks away from Jae and Abel.)

22	**Abel:**	WELL THE SHELL/
23		I EAT IT/

24 **Jae:**   SHELL   *nun*   *mos*   *mek-ci* /
             shell   TOP   cannot eat-right
             (You can't eat the shell, can you?)

25   *ike-n*   *pelyeya-toy/*
             this-TOP   discard-must
             (You should throw this out)

26   *ike*   *man*   *mek-ko/*
             this   only   eat-and
             (and eat only this)

27 **Abel:**   *e/*
             yeah
             (Yeah.)

28	**Jae:**	WE NEED TO COOK IT/
29		PUT THIS RIGHT KID=/

30 **Abel:**   =AND PUT IN *elum* AND WE COULD EAT IT RIGHT=/
             and   put   in   ice   and   we   could   eat   it   right
             (and if you put ice in it you could eat it, right?)

31 **Jae:**   =YEAH/

32   [(unintelligible)

33 **Abel:**   ⌊*ike*   *nemwu*   *ttakttakhay-se*   *mekel*
             this   too   hard-because   eat
             (You eat this because it's too hard)

34 **Jae:**   *mos*   *mekel*
             Cannot   eat
             (You can't eat it.)

35 **Abel:**   *e*   *ttakttakhay/*
             Um   hard
             (Yeah, it's hard.)

36 **Jae:**   [(unintelligible)

37 **Abel:**   ⌊(unintelligible)   *ha-myen*   *cwukel*
                                  do-if   die
             (You die if (unintelligible).)

38	**Jae:**	(emphatically) SPEAK ENGLISH/
39	**Abel:**	OKAY/

40		(touches the head of the snail) OOOOH/
41	**Jae:**	NO LEAVE IT/
42		EY IT'S GONNA GO IN/
43	**Abel:**	IF YOU SCARE HIM/
44		HE'S GONNA GO INTO THE SHELL RIGHT?/
45	**Jae:**	ABEL JUST SEE/
46		(3.5) NOW WE DID MOUTH EYE FEET FEET FEET/
47		FEET FEET LEAVE HIM ALONE LIKE THAT ABEL/
48		IT'S GONNA GO IN/
49		SEE ITS FEET/
50	**Abel:**	(3.5) (softly) IT'S GOING/

I suggested that the codeswitches found in Extract (4.1) at lines 24 and 38 could be analyzed as discourse- and participant-related respectively. In some cases, however, particular contextualizations can be interpreted differently or even be multifunctional. Although the distinction between participant- and discourse-related codeswitching is central to Auer's and to my own analysis, it is important to note that these are not mutually exclusive categories, since some codeswitches may be interpreted as being both participant- and discourse-related (see Extract (4.2) for an example). Auer recognizes the multiple functions contextualized by codeswitching in his demonstration that particular turn-internal switches that contextualize emphasis or reiteration may also be participant-related, in the sense that they reflect the speaker's language competence and his/her interpretation of other participants' reactions. The important point, however, is that discourse- and participant-related codeswitching are not intended to be two generic categories for assembling language alternation types into groups. Rather, they characterize general procedures used as interpretive resources by participants (Auer, 1984: 12).

Codeswitching and task orientation

A brief comment on the relationship between codeswitching and task orientation may be in order. I have noted in the introduction that teachers often frown upon students who use languages other than English in the classroom. The conversational sequences in lines 22 through 37 where Jae and Abel talk about cooking and eating snails may at first appear to be off the given task. After all, the assigned classroom task was to describe and study the snail, not to think of the different ways in which snails can be eaten. However, notice that the boys did not completely go off on an entirely unrelated topic, say, an interesting TV program they had watched, or what they did over the weekend. Rather, they are very much on task as they recount their prior knowledge and experiences with snails. Codeswitching or, more specifically, the use of Korean here enables the children to talk about their experience with snails in the language in which they experienced them. Research in sociolinguistics, language learning and developmental psychology calls for incorporating students' linguistic and cultural knowledge into teaching. Teachers should be urged to 'teach from strengths' by building on what their students know how to say and do and upon the various ways in which children learn, in order to expand the linguistic repertoires of both linguistic minority and majority children (Zentella, 1997: 279).

In the following sections, I analyze participant-related and discourse-related codeswitching separately in greater detail.

Participant-related Codeswitching

Participant-related codeswitching can be divided into two categories: (1) preference-related and (2) competence-related. Preference-related codeswitching allows speakers to let other participants know of their preferences for one language or the other. In the current data, when English was the preferred language of one of the children in the conversation, it almost always overcame the other participant's preference for Korean. In other words, a child who has been speaking Korean might switch to English to adapt to his/her partner's preference for English. But rarely would a child who prefers English switch to Korean to adapt to his/her partner's preference for Korean. In this way, English as the more powerful, socially recognized language in the mainstream classroom was clearly demonstrated in the Korean children's speech. In Chapters 5 and 6, I will show that this asymmetry in power relationships has strong implications for children's bilingual development and maintenance.

Competence-related codeswitching is motivated by the need to adapt to the bilingual proficiencies of other participants. In the current data, more proficient bilinguals moved the conversations along with peers with low proficiency in English by switching to Korean. For instance, among the 12 Korean children, David had made the most recent entrance into the US and had been in this class for only a few months before the time of recording. As a result, he had the weakest command of English of all of the Korean children in the class. The classroom teacher, Mrs Kim, said she almost always had to translate her directions into Korean when David first arrived in her class because he could not understand even the simplest utterances in English.

David's Korean peers also knew of his difficulties with English and would usually switch to Korean to address him. The non-Korean children in the class, particularly the two native English speakers, adapted their speech by speaking more slowly and using gestures and animated facial expressions when speaking with David. One day, one of the native English speakers told David to look at her mouth when she talked so he could understand her better (as though this would make him understand English). This example, however, goes to show that monolinguals and bilinguals alike use their existing communicative resources to get their meaning across to other participants in the conversation. The important point to remember here is that while monolingual English speakers may make use of gestural or prosodic cues to adapt their speech for limited English proficient individuals, bilinguals have the *additional* option of switching their language to achieve the same communicative purpose. In this sense, bilingual codeswitching is a conversational skill to be celebrated and supported, not a sign of incomplete language learning or deficit.

Next I show examples of both types of participant-related codeswitching (i.e. preference-related and competence-related switching) found in the current data.

Preference-related codeswitching: How children negotiate their language preference

In Extract (4.2), we look at an excerpt from a conversation between Joshua and Kwon, who are playing cashier and customer with a toy cash register. At the beginning of this conversational extract, Joshua is annoyed by a jammed cash register drawer, which he has been trying to open. In lines 7 through 30, notice that Joshua speaks only in English while Kwon consistently uses Korean. In line 31, this pattern of competitive language choices ends when Kwon finally gives in and switches to English. In Auer's terms, this constitutes a participant-related codeswitch, whereby Kwon switches to Joshua's preferred language. As in the case of Jae and Abel in Extract (4.1), English again wins out in this sequence, due to its status as the default language in the school context. In this extract and throughout all of the recordings involving Joshua, Joshua's preferred language was English. He hardly ever spoke Korean even when he was specifically prompted to do so. Kwon, in contrast, preferred Korean but whenever he tried to speak Korean, Joshua maintained his use of English, leading Kwon to switch eventually to English also. However, when Kwon was paired with So Hee, who clearly prefers Korean, he produced far more utterances in Korean (see Extract (4.8)).

In the conversational sequence following line 31, both Kwon and Joshua speak English until line 47 when Kwon briefly switches into Korean. This switch, which again appears with a disagreement, may be discourse-related, in contrast to the participant-related switch in line 31. However, Kwon immediately switches back to English in the following utterance and both speakers use English for the rest of the conversation. Again, as in Extract (4.1), participant- and discourse-related switches appear in the same sequence. However, as discussed earlier, some switches are both discourse- and participant-related. For example, Kwon's initial codeswitch into Korean in line 8 may be *both* discourse-related *and* participant-related – while this switch accompanies Kwon's disagreement with Joshua's prior utterance, it also indicates his preference for speaking Korean.

Extract (4.2): Kwon and Joshua play 'cashier'. Joshua plays the cashier and Kwon plays the customer. Joshua struggles with a jammed cash register drawer.

1	**Joshua:**	OH MAN!/
2	**Kwon:**	(3.5) (cash register opens) LET ME SEE (a banging noise)/
3		NO (unintelligible) (a banging noise)/
4	**Joshua:**	(5.5) GERRR-/
5		(1.8) WHY DOES (unintelligible) COME DOWN?/
6	**Kwon:**	(2.0) BECAUSE YOU HAVE TO TOUCH THIS=/
7	**Joshua:**	=NO NO NO NO NO=/
8	**Kwon:**	=*nay nay*/
		(yes yes)
9		(6.5) NO *ceki kinyang neya-toy*/
		no there simply insert-should
		(No, you should just insert there.)
10		(loudly) *kinyang ne!*/
		simply insert
		(Just insert it!)
11	**Joshua:**	I WANT TO PUT (unintelligible)/
12	**Kwon:**	*naol-kkeya*/
		come out-FUT
		(It will come out.)
13		*ilehkey hay*/
		this like do
		(Do like this.)
14	**Joshua:**	⌜(softly) I WANT THE MONEY/
15	**Kwon:**	⌞*ai si*/
		(ah, geez)
16		(3.0) *ai copa copa*/

		ah give give
		(Ah, Give me. Give me.)
17		*ne* *mola* *ne* *mola/*
		you not know you not know
		(You don't know. You don't know.)
18		(4.5) *ai* *si/*
		(Ah, geez.)
19		(1.2) *ya:!/*
		(Hey!)
20		(3.0) *ike* *pwa/*
		this look
		(Look at this.)
21		*iccok* *ey* *nun* *cal* *mos hay-ss-canha/*
		this side at TOP well not do-PAST -not
		(You didn't do it well on this side.)
22		(2.7) *tto* *tto!/*
		again again
		(See you're doing that again!)
23		*a* *si/*
		Ah geez
		(ah, geez.)
24	**Joshua:**	(1.0) IT'S IN HERE/
25		OKAY LET'S GO/
26	**Kwon:**	*ani* *nay-ka ike* *mancess-nuntey* (0.7) *ike*
		no I-NOM this touched-and this
		mancess-nuntey *ettehkey i-ccok-ey lul ka?/*
		touched-and how this-side-LOCACC go
		(Why if I touched this, how come it goes to this side?)
27	**Joshua:**	(1.6) HERE/
28		(1.4) SEE/
29		(1.0) SEE/
30		(unintelligible)/
31	**Kwon:**	SEE?/
32		(6.0) YES!/
33		(banging noise) IT'S BACK OVER HERE/
34		(banging noise) CAN'T FIX/
35		I TOLD YA/
36		LOT OF TIME=/
37	**Joshua:**	=NO SEE/
38		SEE THAT'S GREEN/
39		(1.0) GREEN SEE?/

40		(1.7) (loudly) OOH!/
41		(4.0) THIS GOES (banging noise)/
42		(4.5) YES! (banging noise)/
43	**Kwon:**	(3.0) COME ON YOU'RE TAKING SO LONG=/
44	**Joshua:**	=OK WHAT DO YOU LIKE TO BUY?/
45	**Kwon:**	(loudly) QUIET!/
46		(0.8) AH YOU HAVE IT!/

47		ne	ku-ke	twu-kay	ne	isse-sse/
		you	that-one	two-class	you	have-past

(you, you had two of those.)

48		YOU HAVE SOMETHING NOW/
49	**Joshua:**	QUARTER?/
50	**Kwon:**	YOU HAVE TWO THINGS/
51		TWO (.) BAD (0.9) TWO (.) BIG THINGS/
52		YOU LOST IT WOO—/
53		(3.0) IT'S GONE MAN/
54		(4.0) IT'S GONE/
55		PUT IT BACK/
56		(1.9) NO PUT IT BACK/
57		(picks up a plastic coin) OH! (1.0) I FOUND ONE!/
58		⌜IT WAS LIKE RIGHT OVER/
59	**Joshua:**	⌞IT'S NOT YOURS/
60	**Kwon:**	YES/
61	**Joshua:**	NO/

The important point to remember is that bilingual children use codeswitching to negotiate individual preferences for one language or the other (in this case Kwon for Korean, Joshua for English) and that when the negotiated language of interaction is decided, it is more or less maintained by both participants for the rest of the conversational sequence. We also see that Kwon's initial switch to his preferred language in line 8 can be analyzed as discourse-related in that it contextualizes disagreement in much the same way as the example noted in Extract (4.1). Overall, it is obvious that these six- and seven-year-old bilingual are skillful conversationalists, capable of strategically managing codeswitching to negotiate and accommodate each other's preferences in a way that also structures the ongoing interaction. I turn now to competence-related codeswitching, which is also participant- rather than discourse-related.

Competence-related Codeswitching: Helping peers with low English proficiency

In Extract (4.3), Kathy and David are each given a snail and are asked to create stories with their snails as characters. Notice that this excerpt opens with Kathy and David speaking English. Mrs Kim is standing nearby and listening to their story. In line 1, Kathy asks David which park their snails will go to. After a long delay marked by pauses, David says 'animal park' (line 4). 'Animal park' is a direct translation of the Korean compound noun 'tongmwul-wen' (literally 'animal park') which means 'zoo'. Here, David does not seem to know the English word 'zoo' as indicated by the long delay and his direct translation of the Korean compound noun. Kathy does not seem to understand 'animal park' and asks Mrs Kim to explain its meaning in lines 5 and 6. After David fails to adequately explain 'animal park' in English (lines 7–8, 11), Kathy switches to Korean and presses David to talk (line 12). Mrs Kim is also present at this point. Note that from this point on, Kathy's utterances to David are in Korean. By addressing David in Korean, Kathy seems to have interpreted David's wrong choice of word, long pauses and 'ums' as indicating lack of competence to carry out this activity in English.

However, throughout this conversation Kathy consistently addresses Mrs Kim in English (lines 14 and 28). Therefore, Kathy's codeswitching demonstrates her sensitivity to David's weaker control of English and also to the social norms which require her to use English with Mrs Kim. Later in the same conversation (Extract (4.4) below), Kathy advises David to tell the story in Korean. Such accommodation to the bilingual abilities of the other participant in the conversation has been reported also by Auer (1984: 47) who observed that the Italian–German bilingual children he studied monitored their partner's speech production very carefully for 'mistakes' or insecurities of grammar and pronunciation and adapted their own language choice accordingly.

Extract (4.3): Kathy and David do storytelling with snails.

1	**Kathy:**	WHAT PARK/
2	**David:**	(1.5) UM/
3		(6.5) UM/
4		(4.0) ANIMAL PARK (chuckles)/
5	**Kathy:**	(2.0) (to Mrs Kim) HE SAID ANIMAL PARK?/
6		WHAT IS ANIMAL PARK?/
7	**David:**	UM/
8		(2.0) WHAT (1.0) A RABBIT AND (0.7) UM/

9	**Mrs Kim:**	YOU TELL HER OK?/
10		ALRIGHT NICE AND LOUD YOU TELL HER/
11	**David:**	UM/

12 **Kathy:** (4.5) *ppalli malhay* DAVID/
  quickly talk David
  (Come on. Talk. David.)

13 **David:** (9.0) um/

14 **Kathy:** (5.0) (to Mrs Kim) HE DON'T TALK/

15 **Mrs Kim:** 'KAY/

16 (to Kathy) TELL HIM HE NEEDS TO TALK/

17 **Kathy:** (2.5) *malhay-yatoy/*
  talk-should
  (You should talk.)

18 **David:** *nay-ka mwusun mal hanunci*
  I-NOM what kind talk do
  mollukeysse/
  not know
  (I don't know what kind of thing to say.)

19 **Kathy:** *ne-ka hayyaci nay-ka mwulepo-myen*
  you-NOM do should I-NOM ask-when
  ne-ka mwusun ma-lul hayyaci
  you-NOM what kind talk-ACC do should
  (unintelligible)/
  (You should do it so when I ask, you should say some
  thing (unintelligible).)

20 (4.0) (urgently) *ppalli hay-pwa=/*
  quickly do-see
  (Come on. Try.)

21 **David:** *=alasse/*
  okay
  (Okay.)

22 BACK/

23 (2.3) BACK=/

24 **Kathy:** *=key mwusun mal-iya/*
  that what kind talk-COP
  (What kind of talk is that?)

25 **David:** *e molla na kulehkey ha-myenun*
  Um not know I that like do-if
  (unintelligible)/
  (Um, I don't know if you do it like that (unintelligible).)

| 26 | **Kathy:** | *ne* | *nay-ka* | *cikum mola* | *kulenunci* ale?/ |
| | | You | I-NOM now | something | say Know |

(Do you know what I just said?)

| 27 | **David:** | (1.0) *a* | *mwusun* | PARK *nyakwu malhay-ss-ci/* |
| | | ah | what kind | park COP say-PAST-right |

(Ah. You said what kind of park, right?)

28 **Kathy:** MRS KIM, DAVID DOESN'T KNOW WHAT I'M
SAYING ABOUT/

29 **Mrs Kim:** OK THEN JUST TRY/

30 TRY TO EXPLAIN TO HIM/

31 OK?/

32 YOU'RE DOING A GOOD JOB KATHY/

33 (to David) YOU ARE TOO/

Extract (4.4): Kathy and David continue their storytelling.

| 1 | **Kathy:** | *ne-ka* | *na* | *hantey mola* | *kulay/* |
| | | you-NOM | I | to something | say |

(You say to me something.)

| 2 | | (5.0) *hankwukmal-lo/* |
| | | Korean-with |

(In Korean.)

| 3 | **David:** | *alasse/* |
| | | Okay |

(Okay.)

The codeswitching strategies shown in Extracts (4.3) and (4.4) are similar in many respects to those found in Extract (4.2) in that they are motivated by the need to negotiate the language of interaction. However, the underlying motivation for codeswitching in (4.3) and (4.4) is not preference for a language but rather a limited English competence of one of the participants. If one of the speakers feels uncomfortable in one language, using that language can create confusion and difficulty for both participants in the conversation (as shown in Extract (4.3)). Therefore, the more skilled bilingual speaker usually adapts to the linguistic needs of less proficient speakers. Although students are normally expected to perform activities in English in this classroom, continuing the conversation in English with David would most probably have resulted in severe difficulty or even breakdown of communication.

The role of the first language in acquiring the second language

A brief note about immigrant children's need for first-language help may be in order. Some newly arrived immigrant parents request that their children be placed in mainstream classes without the help of ESL or bilingual classes. They claim that their children will not learn English quickly enough if they are placed in the same class with peers who speak the same first language. Opponents of bilingual education make similar arguments by claiming that students in bilingual education classes are not exposed to enough English and are, therefore, not given the chance to acquire English completely. However, the example in Extract (4.3) shows the potential damage that can be done from insisting that children with little or no English abilities use only English. It is clear from line 27 in Extract (4.3) that David is on task since he clearly seems to know that he needs to explain what kind of park his snail went to. The problem here is that he does not have enough vocabulary in English to carry out the activity entirely in English. Here, without Kathy's adaptation of language, David might have simply given up trying to get his meanings across.

Telling the story in Korean, as Kathy later advised David to do, allowed him to participate in the activity that he would otherwise not have been able to. In fact, allowing language minority students to first tell (or write) their stories first in their first language and translating their work into English has been shown to be an effective method of teaching reading and writing to ESL students (Franklin, 1999). This method assigns legitimacy to both languages in the child's linguistic repertoire and promotes the development of literacy skills in both languages. Supporting the development of biliteracy in immigrant children can be an important empowerment tool and this issue will be discussed in more detail in Chapter 7. However, I turn now to discourse-related codeswitching.

Discourse-related Codeswitching

Participant-related codeswitching as illustrated so far is motivated by a need to negotiate the proper language that is socially appropriate and accommodates all participants' language competences and preferences. Discourse-related codeswitching in contrast, is used to organize the ongoing interaction with respect to such conversational procedures as turn-taking, topical cohesion, sequencing of activities and repair (for an explanation of these procedures, see Atkinson & Heritage, 1984; Levinson, 1983: Chapter 6). Bilingual speakers can make use of codeswitching as a conversational strategy in addition to whatever other strategies are available to monolingual speakers (such as gesture, changes in pitch or tempo – see Couper-Kuhlen and Selting [1996]). The following analysis will focus on four major conversation organizational tasks, all of which have been extensively researched by conversational analysts: (1) turn-taking, (2) preference organization, (3) repair, and (4) procedures for 'bracketing' side-sequences.

Readers interested in a formal discussion on conversation analysis may wish to review Levinson (1983) among other works (Ford & Thompson 1996; Schegloff, 1998; Wells & MacFarlane, 1998) but here I am chiefly interested in illustrating examples in the current data in which codeswitching coordinates some very common conversational organizational procedures. As Auer (1995) notes, an analysis of discourse-related codeswitching avoids the problem of simply listing the discourse functions of codeswitching as discussed in Chapter 1. Most importantly, it makes use of a more general analytic framework to show how codeswitching provides an additional conversational resource for bilingual speakers.

I present, in the following, an example of codeswitching used to contextualize turn-taking.

Using codeswitching to coordinate turn-taking

In Extract (4.5), Kathy and Gina carry out a classroom activity called 'sort by shapes' where they sort and count plastic shapes of various colors and sizes. In line 2, Gina asks Kathy to take her turn in picking out shapes by saying 'your turn' which overlaps with Kathy's *'poca'* (let's see) in line 1. As Kathy does not take her turn at this point (as shown by a two second pause in line 3), Gina codeswitches to repeat her request in Korean in line 4. In line 6, after Kathy once again refuses to take her turn (as shown by a five second pause in line 5), Gina repeats her request yet again and tells Kathy more specifically what to do. However, Kathy still does not take the turn and Gina's next utterance in line 7 boils down to an almost telegraphic speech. Finally, Kathy speaks up and turn transition is completed but instead of doing what Gina asked her to do in line 6, Kathy proposes another task for herself. What is interesting here is Gina's codeswitch in line 4, which is used to coordinate turn-taking. In the literature, such switches have often been said to serve the function of reiteration (e.g. Gumperz, 1982; McClure, 1981).

Codeswitching at turn transition points such as the one shown in line 4 are readily noticeable because it builds up a contrast from the rest of the conversation through the use of a different language from previous turns. In monolingual conversations, turn transitions may be accompanied by changes in pitch or tempo (e.g. louder voice and faster speech) (see Ford & Thompson 1996; Schegloff 1998; Wells & MacFarlane, 1998). When a speaker initiates a question, a request or a command, the next turn speaker may respond in various ways – by remaining silent or by giving a response. If the next turn speaker does not respond immediately, the current speaker may repeat the request as Gina did in Extract (4.5). What is important here is that while monolinguals can use changes in prosodic phenomena such as pitch or tempo to help move along turn transitions, bilinguals have the additional option of switching their languages to help accomplish their conversational goal.

Extract (4.5): Kathy and Gina do 'sort-by-shapes'.

1	**Kathy:**	[*poca/*			
		see let's			
		(Let's see.)			
2	**Gina:**	[YOUR TURN/			
3	**Kathy:**	(2.0)			
4	**Gina:**	*icey*	*ne*	*hay/*	
		now	you	do	
		(Now you do it.)			
5	**Kathy:**	(0.5)			
6	**Gina:**	*ya*	*ne*	*yoko*	*hay/*
		hey	you	this	do
		(Hey, you do this.)			
7		*na ike (.)*	*na*	*ike (.)*	*ne (.)* *ne/*
		I this	I	this	you you
		(I, this. I, this. You. You...)			
		[(unintelligible)/			
8	**Kathy:**	[*ani*	*nay-ka*	*pick*	*hay-yaci* *kunyang/*
		no	I-NOM	pick	do-should simply
		(No, I should just pick.)			

I look more closely now at an issue that has been raised earlier – how codeswitching signals the next turn speaker's responses as preferred or dispreferred.

Using codeswitching to coordinate preference organization

A clear example of the use of codeswitching to signal a dispreferred response (more specifically, a disagreement) was shown in Extract (4.1). A similar pattern of using codeswitching to signal disagreement is illustrated in Extract (4.6). In this conversation, Gina tells a story on the topic 'What can go wrong with some home appliances?' which does not make sense to Kathy. Gina's recurrent repetitions, pauses and a pronoun error (i.e. 'a boy' and 'she') in lines 1 through 4 make the story difficult for Kathy to understand. After Kathy tells her that the story does not make sense in line 5, Gina repeats the last part of her previous utterance in line 6. In line 7, Kathy codeswitches to Korean and repeats that the story does not make sense. Notice that Kathy's complaint (a dispreferred response) in Korean in line 7 contrasts with Gina's English utterance in line 6. Gina then aligns her language choice with Kathy by switching into Korean and insists that her story makes sense in line 8. In line 9, a 2.2-second pause marks Kathy's response as dispreferred as she expresses her dissatisfaction for the third time. Notice that Kathy's language choice (English) is different from that of Gina's immediately prior turn (Korean). Finally, in line 10, Kathy codeswitches once again and complains that she does not understand Gina's story the way it was told.

What is interesting here is that Kathy's dispreferred responses (i.e. lines 7, 9 and 10) are in a language that contrasts with that of the preceding turn. Auer (1984) and Li (1994) provide similar examples in their work with German–Italian and Chinese–English bilingual communities respectively. Their examples as well as the example in this excerpt show that while language alignment is used to express preferred responses, language contrast is used to express dispreferred responses.

Extract (4.6): Kathy and Gina do storytelling on the topic, 'What can go wrong with some home appliances?'

1	**Gina:**	UH UM (0.9) ONE BOY BUY UM (.) UM (0.8) THE UM (0.6) UM REFRIGERATOR/
2		(1.3) AND AND SHE OPENED/
3		AND AND SHE OPENED THE/
4		(2.0) UM (1.0) U:P AND SHE GO- AND SHE AND SHE CAN'T OPEN AND SHE GOES SOMEWHERE AND SHE AND SHE AND I SHE SAW IT AND OPENED/
5	**Kathy:**	THAT DOESN'T MAKE SENSE/
6	**Gina:**	AND THAT OPENED/
7	**Kathy:**	*mal-i an toy:/*
		talk-NOM not make
		(It doesn't make sense.)
8	**Gina:**	*toy/*
		make
		(It does.)
9	**Kathy:**	(2.2) DOESN'T MAKE SENSE/
10		*Mwusun malhay-ssnunci mollukeysse kulay kacikwu=/*
		what kind talk-PAST not know that way
		(Like that, I don't know what you're saying.)

In the next section, I show how codeswitching is used to organize repairs.

Using codeswitching to coordinate repair

In this conversational sequence, I join in on an ongoing conversation between Kyung and Matthew who are buying and selling toy goods in a 'store' activity. In line 1, I point to a cupcake in the 'store' and ask the children in Korean to identify them. Although the children had previously been speaking exclusively in English, they answer my question in Korean, as evidenced by the Korean grammatical morpheme (copula) 'yo'. Structurally, Kyung and Matthew's responses are a second-pair part of an adjacency pair format question/answer. In bilingual negotiations, there is more pressure to accommodate to co-participant's language choice in second-pair parts (e.g. answer) than in first-pair parts (e.g. question) (Auer, 1995). Kyung and Matthew's switch to Korean in lines 2 and 3 shows their accommodation of my use of Korean in the preceding turn.

Extract (4.7): Kyung and Matthew buy and sell toy goods in a 'store' activity. Researcher joins in.

1	**Res:**	*ike-n*	*mwe*	*ya?/*
		this-TOP	what	COP
		(What is this?)		
2	**Kyung:**	CUP	[CAKE	*yo/*
		cup	cake	COP
		(It's a cupcake.)		
3	**Matthew:**	[CUP	CAKE	*yo/*
		cup	cake	COP
		(It's a cupcake.)		
4	**Res:**	*ike*	*nun?/*	
		this	TOP	
		(How about this?)		
5	**Matthew:**	RULER/		
6	**Res:**	*e?/*		
		(what?)		
7	**Matthew:**	RULER=/		
8	**Kyung:**	*=ca*	*yo/*	
		ruler	COP	
		(It's a ruler.)		

In line 4, I point to a ruler and ask the children to identify it. In contrast to his previous response, Matthew offers an answer in English. My question 'e?' (What?) is a 'next-turn repair initiator', which prompts Matthew to either confirm or repair his original response. Notice that this repair initiator is in a language (Korean) that contrasts with the language of Matthew's previous turn (English). Matthew simply repeats his previous utterance in English, refusing to do a repair. Kyung then codeswitches into Korean and repairs Matthew's response. By doing so, Kyung seems to have interpreted my repair initiator 'e?' (What?) as indicating a comprehension problem resulting from Matthew's 'wrong' language choice. In her account of French–English codeswitching practices in Canada, Heller (1982) similarly notes that participants regularly attribute misunderstandings between participants to a problematic language choice.

Using codeswitching to signal side sequences

Codeswitching can be used to signal conversational sequences that are digressions from the main topic at hand. Although pairs structure is pervasive in conversation – such as question/answer and request/concession (or refusal) – various kinds of embedded, non-linear sequences occur which are 'asides' to the main topic. Presequences, insertion sequences and side sequences are all stretches of talk, which occur either before or during the main conversational topic to set the scene or clarify misunderstandings (see further Levinson, 1983). I will illustrate an example of side sequences here, which are examined in detail by Jefferson (1972). A side sequence can occur at an unpredictable point in the conversation. It then picks up where it left off, as shown in Extract (4.8), where So Hee and Kwon are doing a storytelling activity based on the prompt, 'If I had a popcorn popper that never stopped popping popcorn, I would…'. Notice here that a codeswitch brackets off a side sequence from the main body of talk on this topic. The storytelling activity takes place in English, while side comments that organize the main storyline (lines 11, 14, 20–25) are in Korean.

Here, Korean utterances were generally produced much faster than English utterances, supporting Auer's (1995) argument that codeswitching and other contextualization cues (in this case, tempo) often bundle together. In the Korean children's speech data, examples such as Extract (4.8) were fairly common. Giacalone Ramat (1995: 51) discusses a similar example where adult bidialectal speakers use codeswitching as a bracketing device to separate side sequences from the main topic of the conversation.

Extract (4.8): So Hee and Kwon do storytelling on the prompt, 'If I had a popcorn popper that never stopped popping popcorn…'

1	**So Hee:**	IF I HAD A POPCORN POPPER/
		I'LL I'LL GIVE MY CO-(unintelligible)
2	**Kwon:**	IF I GOT A POPCORN/
3		UM UM THERE'S TOO LOT I GO TO THE
		GARBAGE/
4	**So Hee:**	IF I HAD A POP POPCORN POPPER/

5		I'LL GIVE MY PARENTS AND MY MOM
		(unintelligible) A LOT OF (unintelligible)/
6	**Kwon:**	I WISH COULD I HAVE A POPCORN BUT/
7		BUT IF IT IT'S LOT I GIVE TO MY FRIEND/
8		AND AND IF MY FRIEND HAS A LOT/
9		HE THROW IT ON THE GARBAGE (2.0)/
10		UNDER THE GARBAGE (1.3)/
11	**So Hee:**	*Tasi*/
		Again
		(again)
12		I/
13		I'LL EAT THEM WITH MY (unintelligible)/
14		*Hay ca* YOUR TURN/
		do then your turn
		(Do it then. Your turn.)
15	**Kwon:**	IF I GOT A POPCORN/
16		I THOUGHT I EAT IT/
17		IF IT'S A LOT I GIVE IT TO MY FRIEND (1.6)/
18		THEN MY THEN (1.0)/
19		EAT IT/
20	**So Hee:**	*a ya kulen ke epse*/
		ah hey that kind thing not exist
		(ah hey there's no such thing.)
21		SENTENCE *haci-manun ke-ya*/
		Sentence do-not it-COP
		(you're not supposed to do sentences.)
22	**Kwon:**	SENTENCE/
23		*Alasse*/
		(okay.)
24	**So Hee:**	*ne mence hay*/
		you first do
		(you do it first.)
25		*Ppalli=*/
		(quickly.)
26	**Kwon:**	=OK/
27		WHEN I HAVE A POPCORN I EAT IT BUT IF IT'S
		THERE A LOT I THROW IN THE GARBAGE/

I turn now to an issue that was raised earlier – English as the preferred language among the Korean children.

Children's Preference for English

One interpretation of English as the children's preferred medium of communication is that language choice is an explicit statement of an individual's self-perceived identity. Language use in interpersonal interactions is evidence of an awareness of the asymmetrical power relations between the societal and home languages and also between speakers of those languages (Schieffelin, 1994). Immigrant children learn rather quickly the relative position of their native languages in the linguistic hierarchy of American society and respond in a way that would create the least amount of cultural and linguistic conflict. This often means that children learn to prefer English as the medium of communication. While some children's preference for English may be exhibited rather explicitly (as in Jae's command to Abel to 'speak English' in Extract (4.1)), other children's preference for English is displayed in more subtle ways (see Extract (4.2) for Joshua's persistent use of English despite Kwon's numerous attempts to steer the interaction toward Korean). In both cases, however, children who prefer Korean usually yield to their peers' preference for English by switching to English. In this way, codeswitching can also be seen as evidence of the children's enculturation into the language and culture of American society, besides its use as a conversation organizational tool.

Aside from schools, the immigrant family may play a role in some children's preference for English. A child in an immigrant family is exposed to the second language in different ways depending on whether or not he/she is a first-born child. While oldest children in immigrant families learn the second language when they enter school, younger siblings begin speaking the second language before entering school through interaction with the older siblings at home. Second- or third-born children are less often addressed in their native languages than first-borns by parents, get fewer opportunities to practice it and, therefore, tend to become more English-dominant than do first-borns (Shin, 2002a). Besides simply learning the second language earlier, younger siblings are often influenced by the language attitudes of the older siblings (McClure, 1981). Therefore, a child whose older siblings are well integrated into the mainstream community may identify more with the speakers of the dominant language and prefer to be associated more with that group. Interestingly, in the current data, all five children who spoke mostly in English (i.e. Jae, Abel, Joshua, Kyung and Matthew) are either second- or third-born children.

Summary

In this chapter, we saw evidence that far from being a communicative deficit, codeswitching is a valuable linguistic strategy used by bilingual speakers. By comparing the language choice in one utterance against the language choice in the previous turn, the sequential analysis developed by Auer (1984, 1995) showed ways in which the six- and seven-year-old Korean American children use codeswitching to structure their conversation. Very salient in the analysis of the children's bilingual speech, however, was the status of English as the designated classroom language, which led to low overall rates of codeswitching in the data. Five children in particular demonstrated a clear preference for English, which was usually accommodated by their Korean peers who switched to English despite their own preference for Korean. Competing language choices almost always resulted in English prevailing and all participants eventually speaking English. In this sense, codeswitching serves as evidence of the children's socialization into the language and culture of the mainstream American classroom, which discourages the use of languages other than English. Some children clearly lacked competence in English, which was accommodated by their peers who possessed better English skills. The more skilled speakers demonstrated facility in interpreting their peers' insecurities in language production and adapting their language choice accordingly to move the conversation along. Overall, the children made use of every means they had at their disposal, including codeswitching, to negotiate their meanings, intentions and preferences.

With respect to discourse-related codeswitching, we saw evidence that codeswitching is used to coordinate some very common conversational organizational procedures such as turn-taking, preference organization, repair and bracketing of sidesequences. While monolinguals may, for instance, make use of gestural or prosodic cues to organize the interaction, bilinguals have the option of switching to another language *in addition to* using those means that are available to monolingual speakers. In this sense, the children's ability to codeswitch is a valuable linguistic and interactive asset, not an obstacle to their development. The children choose their languages strategically to convey their meanings and do so skillfully and purposefully: the children's codeswitching is a reflection of their self-perception and identity as bilingual speakers (Zentella, 1997) and not a result of an inability to keep the two languages separate.

We have also seen ways in which codeswitching may be used to activate prior knowledge about a given topic and facilitate children's learning of new material. Enabling English-language learners to narrate their prior experience in their mother tongue and helping them to formulate it in the second language is a recommended language development practice for bilingual children (Franklin, 1999). Similarly, insisting that immigrant children use only English in the classroom is counterproductive because it prevents them from making connections to and drawing from what they already know. The presence of languages other than English in the classroom should not be considered as a distraction but as opportunities for growth and learning. Native-language ability is something to be supported, promoted and celebrated rather than be dismissed as hindrance to the development of English.

Chapter 5

Dual Language Development

In this chapter, I explore certain characteristics of the bilingual development of the Korean American children. Growing up as members of the Korean immigrant community in New York City, the Korean American children of this study learned to speak Korean at home and were later introduced to English in school. English is acquired as a second language during childhood while Korean is still continuously developing. Parents and teachers alike are concerned with whether immigrant children can make adequate progress in English acquisition so that they can successfully carry out academic work in English. They often wonder what the children's developing languages look like and whether and how they interact. The goal of this chapter is to address these concerns by looking closely at one aspect of children's acquisition of English morphology, specifically the acquisition of English grammatical morphemes (see Chapter 1 for background literature on morpheme studies).

More specifically, I address the following questions:

(1) Do first-language (L1) and second-language (L2) learners of English acquire the grammatical features in English in the same sequence?
(2) Do L2 learners of English learn the grammatical features of English in the same sequence regardless of L1 background? (i.e. Are there language-specific influences in L2 acquisition?)

In the following sections, I will show that L1 and L2 learners of English do not acquire English grammatical features in the same sequence, which suggests that different processes are at work in L1 and L2 development. Furthermore, I will show that the structure of the L1 influences the sequence of development of L2 grammatical features. However, I show evidence that suggests that the L2 affects certain aspects of the development of the first language as well. I argue that at least certain aspects of the bilingual child's L1 and L2 influence each other as they develop.

The issue of mutual influencing of the two languages in bilingual children's language development is taken up in a separate experimental procedure which analyzes the children's acquisition of the plural morpheme. Following the experimental procedures for eliciting data on the children's use of the plural in Korean and in English (which are outlined in Chapter 3), results of the Korean American children of this study are compared with patterns reported for monolingual English-speaking and Korean-speaking children of the same age. I will show that the Korean American children in most respects follow similar but somewhat of delayed patterns of L1 acquisition of Korean and successive acquisition of English. Related to this, I will discuss crosslinguistic differences in language-acquisition patterns with specific reference to the Korean acquired by the Korean American children. I discuss the implications of the experimental results with respect to the definition of a bilingual speaker established in Chapter 1, as well as to educational policies concerning language minority children in general. But first, I present results of the morpheme study.

Acquisition of Grammatical Morphemes in English

Results of the morpheme study

Figure 5.1 shows accuracy rates achieved by the Korean American children of this study for each English morpheme in descending order. The children scored higher than 90% on seven of the ten morphemes, indicating that they have adequately acquired those grammatical morphemes. However, the three morpheme types that fall well below this level are the article, third person singular -s and the plural. Similar findings are reported by studies that have investigated the patterns of acquisition of English grammatical morphemes by Korean and Japanese speakers. For example, Pak (1987) who examined the acquisition rate of English morphemes by Korean children (ages 5 through 12 years) living in Texas reported that the indefinite article, the third person sing.-s and the plural morpheme were the most difficult for her Korean subjects. Furthermore, Hakuta (1976) showed that scores for the English plural never reached the level of acquisitional criteria during the 13 months of his investigation of a young Japanese child learning English as a second language.[12] As can be seen from the comparisons in Figure 5.1, the Korean children of this study (the New York City children), like the Texas Korean children, experienced particular difficulty with the indefinite article, the third person singular -s and the plural morpheme. But it was the regular English plural morpheme that presented the greatest difficulty for this group as for Hakuta's Japanese subject. Their very low score can be interpreted as incomplete acquisition of this particular grammatical feature, an issue that will be investigated further in an experimental study on plural marking later in this chapter (however, see later in this section for a discussion of Korean phonology regarding word-final /s/).

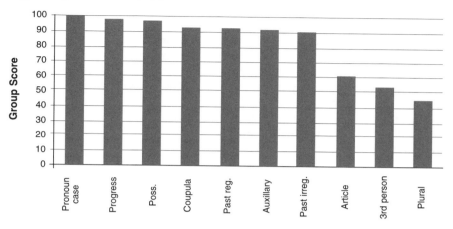

Figure 5.1. Accuracy ranking of English morphemes for 12 Korean subjects

Turning now to errors involving articles, it appears that the absence of this grammatical category in Korean influences its acquisition by the Korean children of this study. Furthermore, the article system is semantically complex in English, encoding a contrast between definite and indefinite reference. It appears from the work of Hakuta (1976) and Fathman (1975) that children whose L1 is Japanese or Korean (neither of which has an article system) have more difficulty learning the English article system than, for example, Spanish-speaking children who have natively acquired a language with an article system. Interestingly, Frauenfelder (1974) reports that English-speaking children in a French immersion program in Canada never confused the definite–indefinite contrast, although they made many errors involving gender on articles – a distinction not present in English. Referring to these findings, Hakuta (1987) argues that it is the absence of a grammatically marked semantic distinction between definite and indefinite reference that causes problems for the Japanese and Korean children, rather than a conceptual problem with this distinction. I provide additional support for this claim in the next section.

The problem with the third person singular morpheme seems to be of a rather different kind, since researchers of both L1 and L2 acquisition of English have found this morpheme to be acquired relatively late (Brown,

1973; De Villiers & De Villiers, 1985; Hakuta, 1976; Dulay & Burt, 1974). Low perceptual salience may be a major factor in its late acquisition by both L1 and L2 learners and it is, moreover, variably deleted in some dialects of English (see for example, Labov, 1972; Cheshire & Milroy 1993). Besides these plausible explanations, a phonological factor other than saliency may also be involved in Korean children's difficulty with the English third person singular agreement marker (as well as the English plural marker discussed earlier) – namely that no words in Korean ever end in /s/. When this phoneme occurs at the end of a word, it is either neutralized to /t/, as in *os* 'clothes' (pronounced [ot]), or is deleted, as in *kaps* 'price' (pronounced [kap]). This could impede Korean children's ability to take note of the English morphemes that are realized as word-final /s/.

In the following section, I compare the results shown in Figure 5.1 with those reported in other studies of English grammatical morpheme acquisition by L1 and L2 learners of English.

Comparison with other morpheme studies

In this section, I address the two questions set out in the beginning of this chapter. The first major issue was whether L2 learners of English acquire the English morphemes in the same sequence as L1 learners. If L2 learners of English acquire the grammatical morphemes in the same sequence as speakers of English as a native language, as some studies have claimed, we should see a statistically similar rank ordering of the grammatical morphemes in Brown's (1973) monolingual English-speaking children and the Korean American children. However, a different rank ordering would suggest that L1 and L2 acquisition do not proceed in the same manner, at least with regard to the set of grammatical morphemes investigated. The second question was whether L2 learners of English acquire the grammatical morphemes in English in the same sequence regardless of L1 background. Implied in this question is whether a child's L1 influences the acquisition of the L2 grammatical features. Following Dulay and Burt (1973) in assuming that accuracy rank reflects order of acquisition, we can compare the rank orders of acquisition of the ten English morphemes for the Korean children with those reported elsewhere.

Table 5.1 shows the rank order for native speakers of English (column English); for Spanish and Chinese children (column Sp.& Ch.)[13]; for a Japanese child (column Japanese); for the Korean children of this study (column NYC K) and for another group of Korean children living in Texas (column Texas K). First, when we compare the order of acquisition for the four L2 groups (Sp. & Ch., Japanese, NYC K and Texas K) to the L1 group

(English), we see clearly different patterns, which supports the claim that children who acquire English as an L2 do not acquire the grammatical morphemes in the same sequence as children who acquire English as an L1 (see Hakuta, 1987; Clahsen, 1990; Meisel, 1991).

When we compare the order of acquisition of the four L2 groups, we see clear differences between the rank orderings reported by Dulay and Burt (1974) (column Sp.&Ch.) and those in the Japanese and Korean studies (Hakuta [1976], current study, and Pak [1987]; columns Japanese, NYC K, Texas K respectively).[14] Hakuta reported that the acquisition order of his Japanese subject was very different from that of Dulay and Burt's subjects (Sp.&Ch.) with a Spearman rho of +0.20 for the nine morphemes that the two studies had in common. Likewise, the results from the Spearman rank order correlation for Dulay and Burt's subjects (Sp.&Ch.) with the NYC Korean children (NYC K) and also with the Texas Korean children (Texas K) show that the accuracy ordering of each of the two Korean groups is significantly different from that of the Spanish and Chinese groups of Dulay and Burt's study.

Table 5.1 Order of acquisition of English grammatical morphemes by first- and second-language learners

	English	Sp.&Ch.	Japanese	NYC K	Texas K
Pronoun case	n/a	1	n/a	1	n/a
Progressive	1	4	1	2	1
Plural	2	5	9	10	8
Past irregular	3	8	7	7	6
Possessive	4	9	2	3	4
Article	5	2	5	8	7[a]
Past regular	6	7	8	5	5
Third person	7	10	6	9	9
Copula	8	3	3	4	2
Auxiliary	9	6	4	6	3

Key: English = Brown (1973); Sp. & Ch. = Dulay & Burt (1974); Japanese = Hakuta (1976); NYC K = current study; Texas K = Pak (1987).
[a] this rank represents a combined average of definite and indefinite tokens (Forth and ninth place respectively).

A series of Spearman rank order tests on the data reported in Table 5.1 revealed the following correlations:

NYC K and English	+0.07 (not significant)
NYC K and Sp. & Ch.	+0.35 (not significant)
NYC K and Japanese	**+0.78 (*p* < 0.01)**
NYC K and Texas K	**+0.90 (*p* < 0.001)**
Sp. & Ch. and Japanese	+0.20 (not significant)
Texas K and Sp. & Ch.	+0.35 (not significant)
Texas K and Japanese	**+0.77 (*p* <0 .025)**

It is clear then that orders of acquisition for the two Korean groups and the Japanese group are similar but that these groups differ from the English, Spanish and Chinese groups. This result is especially noteworthy because the two Korean studies differed from the Japanese study with respect to both data collection and scoring procedures; while both Korean studies were cross-sectional and ordered the morphemes in terms of accuracy of use, the Japanese study was longitudinal and reported a sequential order of acquisition. Presumably, if the data collection and scoring procedures had been uniform across the three studies, the correlation may have been stronger. In any event, the strongest correlation among the five groups in Table 5.1 is found between the two Korean studies (NYC K and Texas K). The fact that the results of these studies converge despite differences in elicitation procedures (Pak employed the Bilingual Syntax Measure [BSM] while the current study used spontaneous speech) strengthens the findings of both. Furthermore, when Pak (1987) is compared with Dulay and Burt (1974), the rank orderings do not correlate significantly even though both studies used the BSM and similar scoring procedures. Both these results have implications for the reliability of the pattern reported for the NYC K children, suggesting that the absence of a significant correlation between the acquisition order of the NYC K children and Dulay and Burt's subjects can not be accounted for by different methodologies. Rather, it is the L1 structures of the different groups of bilingual children, which seem to determine correlation between orders of acquisition.

Since Korean and Japanese are very similar in morphology, syntax and general typological criteria (Martin, 1966; Kim, Y., 1997), the high correlation between the Korean and Japanese rank orders shown in Table 5.1 may further be explained by the similarities between the two languages. Although the historical relationship between the two languages is still controversial, it is likely that Japanese is related to Korean (Martin, 1966). However, Korean is syntactically and morphologically very different from Chinese although it has borrowed numerous Chinese words (Martin, 1992;

see also Chapter 2). And, of course, there is no relationship at all between Spanish and Korean.

Given these facts about morphosyntactic similarities and differences in the languages involved in my comparison, it appears that the child's L1 indeed plays a role in the acquisition of the L2, contrary to the claim that all L2 acquisition is guided by some sort of universal processing strategies. Particularly, given that both Korean and Japanese child learners of English consistently perform poorly on the English article and the plural -s and given that both of these languages lack these grammatical categories, it seems reasonable to conclude that the learner's L1 influences the development of the L2, at least with respect to the acquisition of grammatical morphemes. Vainikka and Young-Scholten (1994) draw similar conclusions regarding the influence of L1 on the acquisition of German phrase structure by adult Korean and Turkish speakers. It is, therefore, surprising that the two groups of children with Spanish and Chinese as L1 backgrounds studied by Dulay and Burt (1974) acquired English morphemes in a similar order, since these two languages are structurally very different (readers interested in an in-depth discussion of these apparently inconsistent findings may wish to refer to Shin and Milroy, [1999]).

Experimental Study on Plural Marking

In this section, I address the issue of interaction between two languages in a bilingual child's repertoire. I discuss the results of the two-part experimental procedure described in Chapter 3 (the interview task and the game task, respectively), which investigated acquisition of the different plural-marking systems of English and Korean. I then discuss the Korean children's language choice patterns as revealed during the experimental procedure, which show ways in which language preference is related to language proficiency.

Results: First (interview) task

The interview task had instructions presented to the children in both English and Korean. Table 5.2 presents the children's responses to the English instruction. The high numbers in column 'Incorrect' shows that most of the Korean children generally do not mark nouns for plural at all. While 'chair' is correctly marked by two children, 'watch', 'sock' and 'block' are each marked correctly by only one child (column 'Correct').[15] The fact that the Korean plural suffix –*tul* is optional may contribute to Korean children's difficulty with the obligatory English plural suffix. The general pattern of no plural marking on either singular or plural nouns can be observed in all of the word items with the exception of 'sock'. Except for one child, all children mark both singular and plural forms of this word as plural (column "Overmark"), probably because 'sock' is more often used in the plural rather than the singular form.

Table 5.2 Response types of 12 Korean American children in the plural marking task (instruction in English)

Word Items	Incorrect	Correct	Overmark
Watch	11	1	0
Chair	10	2	0
Sock	0	1	11
Cat	12	0	0
Tree	12	0	0
Knife	12	0	0
Car	12	0	0
Apple	12	0	0
Block	11	1	0
Snake	12	0	0
Pencil	12	0	0
Camera	12	0	0

Key: Incorrect: no plural marking on either singular or plural noun (e.g. one watch, two watch); and Correct: no marking on singular noun, plural marking on plural noun (e.g. one chair, two chairs); and Overmark: plural marking on both singular and plural nouns (e.g. one socks, two socks)

Table 5.3 shows the children's responses to the Korean instruction. Here, the number of possible response patterns increases to five because some children chose to respond in English while others responded in Korean. Kathy, Kwon, Jae and Gina consistently used Korean for the entire stack of cards while the other eight subjects responded in English with occasional Korean mixed in. However, all 12 children seemed to be aware of the change in the language of the instruction. When the Korean instruction was read, some children explicitly asked if they should respond in Korean. The order of presentation of the stacks did not influence the response patterns – the six children who heard the Korean instruction first did not necessarily produce more Korean responses or more incorrect plural markings in English than the six children who heard the English instruction first.

Table 5.3. Response types of 12 Korean American children in the plural marking task (instruction in Korean)

Word items	Incorrect	Correct	Overmark	Correct K	Incorrect K
Clock	6	1	0	5	0
Table	7	1	0	0	4
Shoe	0	0	8	2	3
Dog	7	1	0	2	2
Flower	7	1	0	2	2
Spoon	8	0	0	1	3
Airplane	7	1	0	2	2
Watermelon	7	0	0	2	3
Ball	6	1	0	1	4
Bird	8	0	0	1	3
Book	7	1	0	1	3
TV	8	0	0	2	2

Key: Incorrect: no plural marking on either singular or plural noun (e.g. one clock, two clock); and Correct: no marking on singular noun, plural marking on plural noun (e.g. one clock, two clocks); and Overmark: plural marking on both singular and plural nouns (e.g. one shoes, two shoes); and Correct K: correct Korean word order (e.g. Noun + Number + CLASS); and Incorrect K: incorrect Korean word order (e.g. Number + CLASS + Noun).

Columns 'Incorrect', 'Correct' and 'Overmark' in Table 5.3 show the same pattern of responses shown in Table 5.2. Although the number of responses for column 'Incorrect' is fewer in Table 5.3, the tendency to avoid plural marking on both singular and plural nouns is still clear.[16] In addition, responses for 'shoe' in column 'Overmark' resemble the pattern for 'sock' in Table 5.2. Similar to 'shoe, 'sock' is more often used in the plural rather than the singular form. Korean responses were either correct (column 'Correct K'), as represented by Examples (5.1) and (5.2), or incorrect (column 'Incorrect K'), as exemplified by (5.3) and (5.4), depending on where the number marker came in relation to the noun.[17] Although Example (5.4) is acceptable with some Korean nouns, Examples (5.1) and (5.2) illustrate the most common order (i.e. Noun + Number + (Classifier)) (Martin, 1992). The word order shown in (5.4) seems to represent a borrowing from English.

(5.1)   *swupak*   *han*   *kay*
          watermelon   one   CLASS
          ('one watermelon')

(5.2)   *swupak*   *hana*
          watermelon   one
          ('one watermelon')

(5.3)*   *han*   *kay*   *swupak*
          one   CLASS   watermelon

(5.4) ?   *han*   *swupak*
          one   watermelon

The incorrect Korean responses show that the bilingual children have some difficulty with Korean classifiers and raise the issue of whether they acquire the classifier system in the same way as monolingual Korean children. Lee (1997) examined the acquisition of a number of Korean classifiers by monolingual Korean children aged two through seven. As discussed earlier in this chapter, Korean has several dozen classifiers that mark different semantic categories of noun in the noun phrase (e.g. *ccak* for shoes, *mali* for animals such as dogs and birds, *songi* for flowers and *tay* for airplanes). Lee found that the number of responses with correct classifiers generally increased with age. In the first part of the experiment where no specific classifiers were provided in the instruction, 67% of the responses of six year olds and 72% of the responses of seven year olds contained correct classifiers. In the second part of the experiment, the children were provided with a classifier in the question and the rate of correct responses increased to 93% for the six year olds and 96% for the seven year olds. Based on these results, Lee concluded that by the age of 7, Korean monolingual children are more or less able to correctly use various Korean classifiers.

Unlike monolingual Korean children, the bilingual children of this study did not produce appropriate classifiers for different classes of nouns. The only classifier that they used for all of the nouns was '*kay*', which, according to Unterbeck (1994) and Lee (1995), is a general classifier covering a wider semantic scope than other Korean classifiers. '*Kay*' co-occurs with nouns referring to small-sized countable objects and replaces other more specific classifiers used with various inanimate objects. For example, the classifier for volumes of papers, '*kwen*' in '*chayk han kwen*' [one book] can be replaced by '*kay*' as in '*chayk han kay*' [one book]. Lee (1995) reports that monolingual Korean children overuse *kay* in the early stages of acquisition and gradually decrease its use as other classifiers are acquired. Given this, it seems that the bilingual children are at an earlier stage of acquisition of Korean as compared with their same-age monolingual Korean peers.

However, the bilingual children do not simply lag in their development of Korean. In addition to overusing the classifier *kay*, the bilingual children produce incorrect word order (i.e. number + (classifier) + noun), a pattern not found in monolingual Korean-speaking children. This is, in fact, an English word order and raises the question of whether this may have been transferred from their knowledge of English. Here we may suspect that not only does the children's L1 influence the course of development of the L2, but the L2 also influences at least certain aspects of the acquisition of the L1. This result is similar to Pfaff's (1993:126) finding that the Turkish development of German-dominant bilingual children is like that of monolingual Turkish children only in some respects – some structures do not develop to the same extent.

Results: Second (game) task

As described earlier, the game task supplements the interview task by eliciting natural speech without experimenter intervention. However, this also meant that a good deal of control over the form of the data was lost. Interestingly, all 12 children chose to carry out the game task in English. One of the difficulties in analyzing the results of this task was that a straight one-to-one comparison with the results of the interview task was impossible. Since I did not intervene, some children spoke much more than their partners. Some children also swapped cards with their partners or sometimes skipped certain items altogether. Despite these difficulties, however, certain general patterns emerged.

First, compared to the interview task (Tables 5.2 and 5.3), more plural nouns were correctly produced in the game task. In the game task, 19 out of the total 24 word items were produced correctly at least 50% of the time. In the remaining five items, the plural was correctly produced 40% of the time or less. As for why the latter five words (i.e. 'knife', 'camera', 'airplane', 'watermelon', 'TV') were more problematic for the bilingual children, there are some plausible explanations. First, 'camera' and 'TV' are English borrowings into Korean and may have been treated as Korean words by some children. 'Knife' has an irregular pluralization (i.e. 'knives', not *'knifes') and the problem with 'airplane' and 'watermelon' may be that they are the only compound nouns in the task. As in the interview task, the items 'shoe' and 'sock' always carried the plural -*s* whether singular or plural was intended.

Since grouping data often hides individual variation (see Andersen, [1978] for a discussion of individual *versus* grouped data), Table 5.4 shows responses to the game task according to individual subject. The 12 children differed widely, as shown by the broad range of the percentage of -*s* marking on plural nouns (14–83%). Eight of the 12 children marked the plural correctly at least 50% of the time while four children scored 43% or below. Understandably, the lowest rate of correct plural marking is seen in David (14%), the least proficient speaker of English among the 12 bilingual children.

Table 5.4. Incidence of *-s* on plural nouns for each subject

Subject	No. of plural nouns spoken	Percentage of -s marking on plural nouns (%)
Abel	12	58
Kathy	7	57
Joshua	7	43
Kwon	8	63
Matthew	18	61
So Hee	8	75
Yooni	11	82
Grace	12	83
Jae	7	43
David	7	14
Kyung	11	55
Gina	5	20

It is worth suggesting here some possible reasons for the children's greater success in correctly marking English plurals in spontaneous speech. Discrepancies between experimentally elicited and spontaneous data are reported elsewhere in the literature (e.g. Marcus, 1995; Marcus et. al, 1992). First, it is likely that interview conditions imposed artificial constraints on the children's responses. In this sense, the game task enabled more spontaneous data to be gathered by reducing the amount of interviewer input and allowing the children to converse freely with one another. It is also likely that the focus on number words and classifiers in the interview task may have reduced the communicative motivation for marking the noun as plural, since I specifically elicited the number words (i.e. 'one', 'two') in each response. These numerals already marked the noun as plural. Be that as it may, note that the rate of correct English plural marking by the bilingual children still falls short of that of the two native English speakers who scored perfectly on all items even in the more constrained setting of the interview task.

The results of both the interview and the game tasks are confirmed by spontaneous speech collected outside the experiment. In free speech, the bilingual children variably marked English plural nouns, similar to the pattern observed in the experimental tasks. Examples such as (5.5), (5.6) and (5.7) were quite common in the monolingual English corpus.

(5.5) Yooni: I like two shape up there.

(5.6) Kathy: Balloon is fifty dollar.

(5.7) Joshua: That'd be hundred dollar.

In acquisitional terms, the variable marking of plurals suggests that the Korean American children have not fully acquired this feature of English grammar. In Chapter 1, I reviewed studies of Turkish children in The Netherlands (Verhoeven & Boeschoten, 1986; Boeschoten, 1990; Verhoeven, 1988; Verhoeven & Vermeer, 1985), which concluded that the bilingual children's development in the two languages is generally slower than the development of Turkish by their Turkish monolingual peers and the development of Dutch by their Dutch monolingual peers. Similarly, the Korean–English bilingual children of the current study lag in the development of their two languages behind both English-speaking and Korean-speaking monolingual children of the same age.

In the next section, I explore the relationship between language choice and language competence, as revealed by the children's responses to the experimental tasks.

Language Choice and Language Competence

Each child who participated in the experimental task selected the response language since neither the Korean nor the English instruction specified which language should be used. The children's choices revealed their language preferences and were skewed in an interesting way. While the Korean instruction elicited some English responses, the English instruction elicited only English responses. It is probable that the children who responded in English to both the Korean and the English instructions selected English as the preferred (and indeed official) classroom language. However, the preference of the children who used some Korean is most plausibly explained not by the effect of situational norms but by a superior Korean competence. In Chapter 4, we saw that codeswitching is motivated by a limited competence in English on the part of one of the participants in the conversation. Similarly, Extract (5.1) below shows examples of codeswitching motivated by a limited competence in Korean by Kyung, one of the most proficient speakers of English among the 12 Korean American children.

In line 1, I elicit Kyung's response for the item 'watch' in Korean. Notice that Kyung's English response in line 2 (i.e. 'one clock') is incorrect since the elicited item is a watch rather than a clock. However, this response is probably related to the fact that the Korean term *sikyey* (watch, clock) covers the semantic range of both 'clock' and 'watch' in English. In line 4, apparently interpreting my repair initiator 'um? (what?)' as a request to switch languages, Kyung reformulates her response in Korean. A three-second gap here probably indicates a processing pause while she remembers the correct Korean word for the item. In line 11, the card with a picture of a table elicits the response *'han uyca'* (one chair). Note that in addition to an English word order (i.e. numeral + noun), which shows the effect of English, Kyung has not produced the correct lexical item, probably due to a gap in her bilingual vocabulary.

After my repeated request for clarification in lines 12 and 13, Kyung attempts to repair her response in English (line 14) but subsequently starts to reformulate her response in Korean (line 15) knowing that a Korean response is required. However, the one-second pause, followed by a switch to English when she offers the word 'desk', suggests that she does not know the Korean word for 'table' and so is unable to complete the utterance in Korean. Referring to switches of this kind, Moffat and Milroy (1992) suggest that one of the motivations for codeswitching in children is to fill lexical gaps in the bilingual vocabulary. In general, Kyung seems to be more comfortable with English nouns as she chooses to respond in English (lines 18, 20 and 22) despite my consistent use of Korean.

Extract (5.1):

1	**RES:**	*ike mwe ya?/*
		this what is
		(what is this?)
2	**Kyung:**	ONE CLOCK?/
3	**Res:**	*um?/*
		(what?)
4	**Kyung:**	I MEAN (3.0) *sikyey/*
		Watch (or clock)
		(I mean watch (or clock).)
5	**Res:**	*um/*
		(yeah)
6		*ike nun?/*
		this TOP
		(How about this?)
7	**Kyung:**	*sikyey?/*
		(watch?)

8	**Res:**	*myech*	*kay*	*isse?/*
		how many	CLASS	is
		(How many are there?)		

9	**Kyung:**	*twu*	*kay/*
		two	CLASS
		(two)	

10	**Res:**	*um/*
		(yeah)

11	**Kyung:**	*han*	*uyca?/*
		one	chair
		(one chair?)	

12	**Res:**	*ikey*	*uyca?/*
		this	chair
		(this is chair?)	

13		(2.0) *uyca*	*ya?/*
		chair	is
		(Is it chair?)	

14	**Kyung:**	I I MEAN/

15		*han* (1.0) I mean one desk?/
		(one)

16	**Res:**	UH HUH/

17		*ike*	*mwe*	*ya?/*
		this	what	is
		(what is this?)		

18	**Kyung:**	TWO TABLE/

19	**Res:**	*Ike-n*	*mwe ya?/*
		This-TOP	what is
		(As for this, what is it?)	

20	**Kyung:**	ONE SHOES/

21	**Res:**	*Ike-n*	*mwentey?/*
		This-TOP	what would be
		(As for this, what would it be?)	

22	**Kyung:**	TWO SHOES/

Kyung's preference for English is shown even more clearly in Extract (5.2) where after she responded in English to questions in Korean, I explicitly direct her to speak Korean (line 3). Note that in line 6, the mixed utterance 'two *swupak*' (two watermelons) again shows the effect of English word order (i.e. number + noun). From line 9, all of Kyung's responses are in English for the rest of the session and my several attempts to induce her to respond in Korean are apparently unsuccessful as Kyung repeatedly goes back to using English. Thus, language preference associated with a greater competence in English seems to have largely determined language choice in Kyung's case. However, the role of the interlocutor in determining language choice is also important. It is quite possible that the children's knowledge of my bilingual abilities affected the outcome of the experiment. Had a monolingual Korean speaker administered the Korean portion of the test, more Korean responses may have resulted.

Extract (5.2):

1 **RES:**   *Ike-n?/*
               This-TOP
               (As for this one?)
2 **Kyung:**   A WATERMELON/
3 **Res:**   *hankwukmal lo   mal-halay?/*
               Korean   in   talk-would
               (Would you talk in Korean?)
4 **KYUNG:**   *swupak/*
               (watermelon)
5 **Res:**   *um/*
               (yeah)
6 **Kyung:**   TWO *swupak/*
               (watermelon)
7 **Res:**   UH HUH/
8   *Ike-n   mwe ya?/*
               This-TOP   what   is
               (As for this, what is it?)
9 **Kyung:**   UM (2.5) ONE BALL?/
10 **Res:**   UH HUH/
11   *Ike nun?/*
               this TOP
               (How about this?)
12 **Kyung:**   TWO BALL/

Next, I explore the issue of whether the Korean American children's error-ridden acquisition of English and relatively error-free acquisition of Korean may be explained by the inherent structural differences in the two languages.

Crosslinguistic differences in language acquisition

Crosslinguistic investigations of L1 acquisition (e.g. Slobin, 1985/1992, 1997) have identified significantly different patterns of development in morphosyntactic marking of parallel constructions by children acquiring different languages. When we examine the Korean children's patterns of use of inflectional morphology in Korean, we find that they are very similar to those of monolingual Korean-speaking children of the same age. This is true even for the English-dominant children in this study who make very few errors in Korean morphology in areas such as case and tense–mood–aspect marking. However, we have seen that the Korean children acquire English grammatical morphemes in an order very different from that reported for monolingual English-speaking children. Aside from the fact that the children of this study are acquiring English as an L2, inherent structural differences in the two languages may explain differences in patterns of language acquisition.

Language-acquisition studies of monolingual Korean children indicate that Korean-speaking children have no difficulty in producing both verbal inflections and nominal particles [18] (Kim, 1997). Kim reports that a variety of verbal inflectional affixes expressing different tenses, aspects, moods, modalities, conjunctions and speech levels are used productively before two years of age and errors in the use of verbal inflectional endings are generally rare, if not totally absent. Verbal inflectional endings are present in the one-word stage and children do not make errors in the serial order of inflections. Kim (1997) also notes that children acquiring Korean as a native language begin to produce adult forms of negation as early as 1:7 and, by the beginning of the third year, they use distinct lexical forms of negation to express different semantic functions such as non-existence, prohibition, rejection, denial, inability and ignorance. In addition, the emergence of relative clauses in children's production samples is early compared with reports from other languages; Korean children begin to produce relative clauses at around 2:0. The acquisition of complement phrasal constructions is also early: Korean children productively use different infinitival complement constructions between the ages 1:9 and 2:5. The bilingual children of the current study generally follow these patterns.

Kim (1997) notes that, in general, Korean children's speech at very early stages is very similar to that of Korean adults, compared with children learning other languages such as English. If all children are born equipped with Universal Grammar, then why does it take considerably longer for English-speaking children to produce adult-like speech than for young Korean speakers acquiring Korean? It is suggested that the adult grammars of English and Korean may differ in crucial syntactic aspects, most probably with respect to functional categories (Kim, 1997: 436). Kim reasons that if some functional categories are absent or are syntactically inactive in Korean adult grammar –for example, if the nominative CASE is not assigned by INFL as in English but by default – some of the differences in the acquisition patterns between Korean and English would be readily accounted for.

A similar pattern of crosslinguistic differences in language acquisition is found by Pfaff (1993) who reports that her Turkish–German bilingual subjects followed a pattern of Turkish L1 acquisition with a successive acquisition of German. While the children's acquisition of Turkish proceeded essentially on the lines that have been reported for Turkish monolinguals, their acquisition of German differed strikingly from that reported for German monolinguals and was, in some respects, similar to the patterns characteristic of natural second language acquisition of German by adults and older children. In addition, she found that the Turkish-dominant children's inflectional morphology was almost identical to that of Turkish monolingual children and even the German-dominant children in her studies made fewer errors in Turkish morphology than in their German morphology. Pfaff attributes the differences in the children's acquisitional patterns of Turkish and German to the relative opacity of German morphosyntax as compared to Turkish morphosyntax (which is generally much more regular). Similarly, the Korean American children's almost error-free acquisition of Korean (except for word order in the noun phrase as discussed in the previous section) and error-ridden acquisition of English appear to be influenced by the inherent structural differences between those two languages.

Summary and Discussion

In this chapter, I explored certain characteristics of the bilingual development of the Korean American children. I first examined the Korean American children's use of English grammatical morphemes. Contrary to the claim that L2 acquisition follows the same sequential path regardless of the speakers' L1 background, cross-study comparisons show evidence which suggests that L1 structures influence the course of L2 acquisition. For example, there were clear differences in rank order of acquisition of English morphemes between Spanish-speaking and Chinese-speaking children on the one hand (Dulay & Burt, 1974) and Korean-speaking children on the other. However, the rank orders of the Japanese child and the two groups of Korean-speaking children correlated at a statistically significant level. Given the fact that Korean and Japanese are structurally very similar, this result suggests that there are language-specific influences on L2 acquisition. Thus, whether or not these young learners continue to access Universal Grammar principles as L1 learners do, their L2 acquisition strategies appear to be affected by the knowledge they have acquired of their L1.

I also presented evidence that suggests that young immigrant children temporarily lag in their grammatical development of both of their languages. Results of the experimental study on plural marking revealed that the Korean children generally do not mark English nouns for plural. Since monolingual English-speaking children of a similar age produced the plural forms correctly, it was concluded that the Korean–English bilingual children have not, at least in this respect, reached the level of acquisitional maturity of their monolingual English-speaking counterparts. Similarly, the Korean American children were found to fall short of full acquisition of the Korean classifier system. For example, while monolingual Korean-speaking children of similar age are reported to be producing various classifiers in Korean, the Korean American children produced only *kay*, a general classifier which is documented to be overused in early stages of monolingual Korean children's acquisition of Korean classifiers. Since bilingual children use the two languages in different circumstances (e.g. Korean at home, English at school), it is not surprising that they are not on a par with monolingual children in terms of grammatical development in those languages. The observed delay is somewhat expected, given that a bilingual is rarely equally or fully proficient in two languages.

One confounding factor in this overall pattern of delayed acquisition of Korean, however, is the children's management of word order in the noun phrase involving numeral and classifier. Specifically, while the acquisition of the semantics of classifiers is generally unaffected by the bilingual children's knowledge of English, variant word order in Korean is influenced by the children's knowledge of English word order. Thus, the L2 seems to influence the development of the L1 grammatical features at least in some ways. Since the Korean American children appear generally to follow a pattern of L1 acquisition of Korean and L2 acquisition of English, this exception may suggest that word order acquisition patterns need to be considered separately. At any rate, a child L2 learner is qualitatively different from an adult L2 learner in that s/he is still in the process of acquiring the L1 while learning the L2.

The observation that bilingual children fall behind in their linguistic development (albeit temporarily) as compared to same-age monolingual children has often been misinterpreted to indicate that bilingualism hurts children. Results like the ones shown in this chapter can be misused to argue that it is counter-productive to the child's welfare to develop and maintain proficiency in more than one language since learning two languages seems to retard development in both languages. However, one must remember that young bilingual children are continually developing in their two languages and the results presented in this chapter are only a snapshot of their development at a particular moment in time. The fact that bilingual children's knowledge of English has not currently caught up with that of same-age monolingual English-speaking children should not be taken to mean that their delay is going to be permanent. Most of these children have been speaking English for less than three years and, therefore, have not had the chance to fully catch up with their monolingual English-speaking peers in terms of their English development. With time, however, the children are likely to command skills and competence in English comparable to native English speakers.

What is reasonable in terms of the amount of time required for L2 acquisition by immigrant children? In Chapter 1, I discussed that at least five years are required for immigrant children to attain grade norms on academic aspects of English proficiency (Collier, 1987; Cummins, 1981; Klesmer, 1994; Ramirez, 1992). Even students in additive bilingual settings such as the Canadian immersion programs tend to lag behind their monolingual peers for a short period in academic achievement. However, once they acquire L2 proficiency sufficient to operate in a cognitively demanding and context-reduced environment, they normally catch up with their peers (Baker & Prys Jones, 1998). Although there is compelling research evidence that suggests that bilingual language acquisition requires time, rapid transition of language minority students into English-only instruction is what is increasingly demanded of teachers, students and parents (for more on the societal pressures to shift to English, see Chapter 6). Because of these pressures, many linguistic minority children are mainstreamed before they are ready and fall progressively further behind grade norms in the development of English academic skills (Cummins, 1996).

The question of whether and when the Korean American children will catch up with their monolingual counterparts in both Korean and English in terms of grammatical development depends on many psychosocial, cultural and educational factors. In fact, it is unlikely that the two languages will develop equally, as the children are growing up in an environment where one language is particularly valued and promoted while the other one is systematically devalued. As was shown in Chapter 4, the children have a clear perception that English is the language of the classroom and that Korean is particularly discouraged in the school. The early-exit transitional bilingual education program in which the Korean children are enrolled at this school is what Skutnabb-Kangas (2000) refers to as a 'weak model of bilingual education'. Although such programs are a more 'humane' way of assimilating language minority students, the goal is nevertheless assimilation and strong dominance in the majority language. Skutnabb-Kangas states that early-exit transitional programs show often better results than submersion programs in terms of student achievement but the positive results are often limited to psychological gains: self-confidence, security, better home–school cooperation. Often the programs are phased out so early that they make virtually no difference to the children's school achievement or linguistic competence in the mother tongue and the second language.

Given this subtractive bilingual context, it is expected that the Korean American children would speak increasingly smaller amounts of Korean. The children's current errors in English grammar are likely to disappear as they become fully competent in English while their ability in Korean is likely to weaken progressively until eventually they can claim only a passive knowledge of their native language. Since few Korean American children have access to adequate heritage-language maintenance support mechanisms, many are likely to lose proficiency in Korean and become English-dominant.

In the next chapter, I discuss factors that contribute to an overall shift to English in Korean American families.

Chapter 6

Pressures for Language Shift

> You want to speak to your children in your own language; you want to talk about certain topics from your heart, but it's hard when you can only speak broken English. (Quoted in Cho, 2001).

In Chapter 4, we saw that there is a clear perception among the Korean children that English is the language of authority and power, endorsed by the school. Some children's preference for English can be interpreted as an explicit statement of their self-perceived identity and evidence of an awareness of the differential power relations between English and Korean. Immigrant children experience tremendous pressure to abandon their native languages in favor of English. However, the pressure is not only felt by children but also by parents who may promote the use of English at home for a variety of reasons. Parents' attitude toward the two languages significantly influences the ways in which they socialize their children to view, learn and use them. The ways in which children are socialized to use their two languages in turn have a strong impact on whether they will grow up to be bilingual or monolingual. In this chapter, I examine parental language attitude and family literacy practices in the Korean American community and present a case for heritage-language development and maintenance among immigrant children.

Specifically, I explore personal, social and educational pressures to shift to English and abandon Korean. I present evidence that parents' emphasis on education and desire to see children develop fluent and unaccented English contribute greatly to an overall shift to English in the Korean American family. I also discuss the consequences of poor advice given to parents by ill-informed teachers, doctors and speech therapists to stop speaking Korean at home for the sake of the children. Furthermore, I examine ways in which English-only policies and the current national emphasis on educational testing drive parents to abandon the transmission and maintenance of their native language.

I start by presenting factors that contribute to language shift in the

Korean American family as revealed in the responses to the survey questions and interviews (see Chapter 3 for descriptions of these procedures).

Survey Respondents' Background

A summary of the survey respondents' characteristics is presented in Table 6.1. The great majority of the questionnaire respondents were women – 190 out of the 251 surveys were completed by females while the rest were completed by males. The respondents ranged in age from 32 to 54, with a mean age of 42 years. Length of residence in the United States as reported by the respondents ranged from 2 to 28 years, with 16.5 years as a mean length of residence. Over three-quarters of the sample have lived in the US for more than 10 years. Respondents' age at arrival in the United States ranged from 10 to 43 years of age, with 25.6 years as the mean age. The majority of the respondents had arrived in the US in their twenties (66.8% of the sample) whereas 11.9% had arrived in the United States as teenagers (range: 10 – 17 years of age) and 21.3% had arrived when they were 30 years of age or older. 68.5% of the families in the sample have two children each, while 16.3% of the families have three children and 15.1% have a single child.

Table 6.1 Summary of survey respondent characteristics

Sex	Female (76%); Male (24%)
Current age	32–54 years old (mean: 42)
Length of US residence	2–28 years (mean: 16.5)
Age at arrival in the US	10–43 years old (mean: 25.6)
Number of children	1 (15.1%)
	2 (68.5%)
	3 (16.3%)
Education	College + (81.2%)
	High school (18.8%)

By and large, the respondents were highly educated. A remarkable 81.2% of the parents surveyed had received either college or graduate degrees, while the rest were high school graduates (18.8%). These numbers far surpass the figures for the general Korean American population in the US – in 1990, 55% of Korean Americans 25 years of age or over had some college education and 80% had at least a high school education. Despite the remarkably high levels of education, about half of the respondents reported their listening, speaking and writing skills in English to be 'not good.' The respondents, however, generally reported having better reading skills in

English – more than two-thirds of the parents reported their reading skills in English to be 'good' or 'very good'. These responses may reflect the largely text- and translation-driven English instruction that the respondents had received in Korea (Kim *et al.*, 1980).

As shown in Table 6.2, length of residence correlated significantly with level of reported English skills – the longer the residence in the US, the higher the reported English abilities. Level of education also correlated significantly with English abilities – better-educated individuals generally claimed higher English proficiency. Furthermore, age at immigration showed significant negative correlation with English abilities – respondents who had immigrated at an earlier age generally reported higher proficiency in English. There was a clear sex difference in English abilities as well. The male respondents generally reported higher abilities in English in all four skill areas than did the female respondents, which may be related to the fact that the men in the sample tended to be better educated than the women. In fact, sex and level of education were significantly correlated ($p<0.05$).

Of the respondents, 95.3% reported that they attend a Korean church regularly and 86.7% said they use Korean with fellow church congregants.[19] This is in accord with Kim & Hurh's (1993) finding that regardless of length of residence, Korean immigrants retain close social ties with members of their ethnic group. However, note that this result may have been skewed by the methodological design of the survey, which was distributed primarily in Korean American churches.

Table 6.2 Pearson correlation coefficients for respondents' demographic data and English abilities

	Listening	*Speaking*	*Reading*	*Writing*
Length of residence	0.587[b]	0.589[b]	0.516[b]	0.440[b]
Education	0.416[b]	0.380[b]	0.512(b)	0.412[b]
Age at immigration	-0.403[b]	-0.353[b]	-0.331[b]	-0.270[b]
Sex	-0.166[a]	-0.205[b]	-0.218[b]	-0.277[b]

[a] $p<0.05$; (b) [b] $p <0.01$.

Effects of Schooling on Language Shift

In Chapter 1, I discussed that children's motivation to speak English at school is often the initial driving force for language shift in the immigrant family, as English is brought home. In the current survey administered to Korean American parents, the effects of schooling on children's language use were clearly evident in the responses to the questions about the language each child spoke with the parent before and after entering school (see Table 6.3). The children, across birth-order categories, spoke more English (or mixed Korean and English) and less Korean with their parents once they entered school. However, even before entering school, fewer second-born children (66.3%) than first-born children (78.8%) spoke Korean with their parents, while even fewer third-born children (42.9%) did so. Instead, before entering school, later-born children generally spoke more English (or more mixed Korean and English) than did first-born children. Similar pattern is reported by Hakuta and D'Andrea (1992), who found that the earlier Spanish-speaking Mexican immigrants began learning English, the lower their levels of proficiency in English. Similarly, later-born children generally learn English at an earlier age than do first-born children through exposure to English brought home by first-borns (Fishman, 1991; Shin, 2002a; Wong Fillmore, 1991; see also Valdés, 1996).

Table 6.3 Language each child spoke with parents before and after entering school (%).[a]

Language(s)	First-born child (n=204)		Second-born child (n=204)		Third-born child (n=41)	
	Before	*After*	*Before*	*After*	*Before*	*After*
Korean	78.8	34.1	66.3	26.8	42.9	23.8
K and E	16.5	50.6	24.1	53.7	33.3	42.9
English	4.7	15.3	9.6	19.5	23.8	33.3
Total 100	100	100	100	100	100	

[a]In this table, respondents with one child were excluded.

Language Use in the Immigrant Family

Survey results indicate that language shift is well underway in the Korean American family. While the respondents reported speaking almost exclusively in Korean with their parents (grandparents' generation), they use slightly more English with their spouses and still the most amount of English with their children (Tables 6.4 through 6.6). The mother and/or father take care of the children in 77.4% of the families while the grandparent(s) provide childcare in the remaining families: there are very few families where a non-relative takes care of the children. There are clear differences in language use patterns as exhibited by adults and children. The language most often used by the caretaker(s) in speaking to the children is Korean (56.1%) or mixed Korean and English (37.8%). Only 6.1% of the caretakers use English solely in communicating with the children. In contrast, most children use English (74.7%) or mixed Korean and English (19.8%) to speak to themselves when playing alone. However, when children ask their parents for something they want (e.g. money, new toy), they generally use more Korean – 20.7% use only Korean whereas 43.2% use mixed Korean and English. Of the children, 36.1% use solely English when asking their parents for something they want.

Table 6.4 Language respondents use when discussing personal and domestic matters (%)

	Korean	*K and E*	*English*	*Total*
With parents	96.1	3.9	0	100
With spouse	84.5	15.5	0	100
With children	31.8	61.2	7.1	100

Table 6.5 Language respondents use when discussing current happenings in Korea (%)

	Korean	*K and E*	*English*	*Total*
With parents	95.9	4.1	0	100
With spouse	91.6	7.2	1.2	10
With children	28.2	55.1	16.7	100

Table 6.6 Language respondents use when discussing current happenings in the US

	Korean (%)	*K and E (%)*	*English (%)*	*Total (%)*
With parents	95.9	4.1	0	100
With spouse	76.8	18.3	4.9	10
With children	21.3	56.3	22.5	100

When parents and children communicate, both parties make use of a number of strategies to accommodate each other's language competences and preferences. For example, when children talk to their parents in English and parents fail to understand them, most parents ask their children to repeat what they said or to speak in Korean (see Question (1)). Children also try to accommodate their parents' language preferences and competences by switching to Korean or by slowing down their speech (see Question (2)). Other children, particularly those who have low proficiency in Korean, continue using English but speak more slowly or use simpler terms in English to communicate their meaning. However, these latter strategies do not always help, as some parents still do not understand their children's English utterances. After repeated unsuccessful attempts to get their meanings across, some children become frustrated and give up trying entirely, saying 'never mind' (14.7%).

Question (1): When your child speaks to you in English and you don't understand, what do you do?
- Ask to explain/say it again. (51.9%)
- Ask to speak in Korean. (30.8%)
- Ask to speak more slowly. (5.8%)
- Such thing has never happened. (4.8%)
- Get the children's father to help. (2.9%)
- Ask to write it down. (1.9%)
- Ask my eldest child to interpret. (1%)
- Look up the word in the dictionary. (1%)

Question (2): When your child speaks to you in English and you don't understand, what does your child do?
- Tries to explain it in Korean. (33.7%)
- Says it again more slowly. (30.5%)
- Gives up after trying to explain it again, or says 'never mind.' (14.7%)
- Explains in simpler terms in English. (13.7%)
- Such thing has never happened. (3.2%)
- My eldest child explains. (2.1%)
- Tries to look up the word in the dictionary. (1%)
- Spells out the word for me. (1%)

Language Attitude of Parents

By and large, Korean parents are aware of the value of bilingualism and would like their children to be proficient in both Korean and English. Most parents see the home as a domain for Korean use – 63% reported that they would like their children to use Korean and 36% stated that they would like children to use mixed Korean and English. However, parents generally want children to use English outside the home (40%), or mixed Korean and English (50%). In general, while parents accept their children's preference and need for speaking English, they also seem to be deeply interested in children's maintenance of Korean. Three-quarters of the respondents want to send their children to Korea at some point to study Korean while over four-fifths of the parents would like to see Korean offered as a foreign language subject in US public schools.

When asked about their views on children speaking English among themselves at home, most parents were either positive or neutral. Only a small minority (14%) did not like their children speaking English among themselves. Some of the parents who reported having positive attitudes toward their children speaking English stated that younger children benefit from learning English through interaction with their older siblings at home. When asked a related question about children using mixed English and Korean when addressing their parents, most parents were again either positive or neutral. Only 12% of the parents reported that they do not like their children addressing them in both Korean and English. In fact, many parents seem to view this as an opportunity to learn English from their children. However, most parents want their children to speak Korean when Korean-speaking friends or relatives are present – only 9% of the parents surveyed said they feel good about children speaking English in the presence of their Korean-speaking friends or relatives.

For a further understanding of the respondents' attitudes toward bilingualism, a series of chi-square tests of independence was performed to examine the relationships between various measures of the respondents' attitudes toward their children's bilingual development and their demographic backgrounds (see Table 6.7). For this test, the respondents were dichotomized by each of the following variables: (1) length of residence by the mean year (less than 16.5 years, more than 16.5 years), (2) education (college graduates, non-college graduates), (3) age at immigration by the mean year (less than 25.6 years old, more than 25.6 years old) and (4) sex.

Parents' attitude toward the use of English was generally related to the amount of exposure they have had in English. As shown in Table 6.7, length of residence is significantly related to the respondents' desired home language – the longer the repondents have lived in the United States the more they would like their children to speak English at home. Furthermore, parents who had immigrated to the US at an earlier age tend to favor greater use of English by their children both at home and outside the home. These responses may be explained by the fact that the amount of parents' experience with English usually increases with increasing years of residence in the US, resulting in greater proficiency and comfort level in that language. Likewise, some of the parents who had immigrated to the US at a relatively young age have had the opportunity to be schooled in English, which may explain their tendency to prefer English. Aside from parents' desired language for their children, proportionately more women than men showed interest in seeing Korean offered as a foreign language subject in public schools.

Table 6.7 Chi-square tests of independence between demographic variables and parental attitude toward children's language development

	Desired home language (Korean, K and E or English)	Desired outside language (Korean, K and E or English)	Want to send children to Korea to learn Korean	Want Korean as a foreign language subject
Length of residence	18.720[c]	2.913	0.000	0.384
Education	2.805	0.721	3.294	0.539
Age at immigration	12.715[c]	11.768[c]	2.585	0.123
Sex	0.700	2.242	2.8	6.481[a]

[a] $p<0.05$; [b] $p<0.01$; [c] $p<0.005$

The overwhelming attitude among the parents is that Koreans in America should be proficient in both Korean and English. For example, when asked what they think about Koreans in the US who cannot speak Korean, 82.4% of the respondents stated that it is bad, shameful, or unacceptable while 17.6% said it is okay or understandable (see Question (3)). When asked what they think about Koreans in the US who cannot speak English, even a higher proportion of the sample think that it is bad, problematic or shameful (90.1%) (see Question (4)). Compare, however, the top two responses to Question (4), 'They should learn English' (45.8%) and 'It poses problems for living in the US' with the top two responses to Question (3), 'It's not good' (24.4%) and 'I feel sorry for them' (22%). Rather than stating that lack of English skills is bad, the majority of the respondents chose to focus on the practical *need* to learn English to live in America. However, lack of Korean skills by a Korean person living in the United States is judged based on the intrinsic value of knowing an ethnic language and not based on its need for day-to-day living. A small number of the respondents who reported that it is acceptable for a Korean living in the States not to speak English stated that long working hours prevent them from attending English language classes. In general, most respondents seem to be well aware of the many problems associated with one's lack of abilities in English, which leads to embarrassment, inability to exercise one's rights adequately, and being perpetually perceived as a foreigner by Americans (see also Krashen, 1998).

Question (3): What do you think about Koreans living in the United States not able to use Korean?
• It's not good. (24.4%)
• I feel sorry for them. (22%)
• It's shameful. (16.1%)
• They need to learn Korean. (16.1%)
• It's understandable if the person has lived in the US for a long time. (15.5%)
• It's their parents' fault. (3%)
• It doesn't really matter. (1.8%)
• I don't think they're Korean. (1.2%)

Question (4): What do you think about Koreans living in the United States not able to use English?
• They should learn English. (45.8%)
• It poses problems for living in the US (16.3%)
• It's not good. (9.6%)
• I feel sorry for them. (7.2%)
• It's understandable. It depends on the situation. (6%)
• It's shameful. (5.4%)
• It's unacceptable. (5.4%)
• It's understandable since English is difficult to learn. (3.6%)
• They're not Korean. (0.6%)

In sum, children's development into proficient bilinguals is the outcome most desired by parents since bilingualism allows children to operate in both languages and 'get the best of both worlds'. Parents themselves aspire to become bilingual and are convinced that English ability is critically essential for life in the United States. However, we shall see that, for most Korean American families, bilingualism is not so easy to attain.

Literacy Practices at Home

Most of the respondents reported that they teach Korean to their children (82%). This is not surprising since parents are often the most significant source of Korean input for children. However, only 55% of the respondents read to their children in Korean. This may be due to a general lack of children's books in Korean at home (Scarcella & Chin, 1993). Studies of various immigrant groups show that language minority students in the US generally have very limited access to native-language reading materials at home, in school and in the community (McQuillan, 1998; Pucci, 1994). My observations also show that good quality, age-appropriate printed materials in Korean are in short supply in many Korean American homes.

Since more access to books leads to more reading and more reading leads to higher levels of literacy (Krashen, 1993), one of the requirements in developing Korean literacy is increasing access to interesting, comprehensible Korean texts (see also Chapter 7 for suggestions on how to make heritage-language reading materials more widely available).

Compared to literacy practices in Korean, activities that promote the development of English literacy skills display a different pattern. The survey results showed that only 29% of the parents reportedly teach English to their children. This is not surprising since the respondents generally reported low levels of English proficiency. However, despite their lack of English skills, more than half of the sample reported that they read to their children in English (55%). In addition, almost half of the parents reported helping children with their homework in English (46%). It therefore seems that children's development of English literacy skills is a higher priority for many Korean parents than their development of Korean literacy skills. This is probably due to the fact that English is closely linked to school performance whereas Korean is not (see also Chapter 2 for the relationship between educational opportunities and Korean immigration to the US).

When we examine the results more carefully, we find that length of residence, age at immigration and education are significantly related to the proportion of respondents who teach and/or read English to their children at home (see Table 6.8). This may be due to the fact that all of these variables are related to parents' level of English proficiency (i.e. respondents with longer US residence, lower age at immigration and higher education level report being more skillful in English; see Table 6.2). Parents with longer and more extensive exposure to English tend to use more English with children at home. Parents with longer exposure to English also tend to perceive themselves as more American than those with shorter stays in America. In regards to self-perceived identity, 50% of the respondents stated that they consider themselves to be Korean while 48.8% consider themselves to be Korean-American. Length of stay in the US was strongly correlated with the respondents' self-perceived identity – the longer the respondents have lived in the US, the more American they considered themselves to be ($\chi^2 = 35.402$, $p = 0.000$). Furthermore, level of education correlated significantly with the respondents' perception of their identity – the more educated the respondents are, the more American they viewed themselves ($\chi^2 = 30.272$, $p = 0.000$). However, neither age at immigration nor sex correlated significantly with the respondents' view of their identity.

Table 6.8 Chi-square tests of independence between demographic variables and parental efforts toward literacy development in children

	Send children to Korean school	Teach Korean to children	Read in Korean to children	Teach English to children	Read in English to children
Length of residence	0.698	0.729	3.691	9.173[c]	5.875[a]
Education	1.129	3.523	0.404	4.155[a]	0.966
Age at immigration	1.091	0.002	0.049	16.092[c]	17.051[c]
Sex	1.500	0.199	0.001	0.052	0.481

[a] $p<0.05$; [b] $p<0.01$; [c] $p<0.005$

Of the parents, 42% reported that they send their children to weekend Korean language schools. This relatively high rate of attendance in Korean language schools (compared to about 13% attendance rate among second-generation Korean-Americans nationwide) may be explained by the fact that the respondents were solicited through Korean American churches, many of which are affiliated with Korean language schools. In addition, the questionnaires may have been returned more by parents who are interested in children's Korean development. However, parents who send their children to weekend Korean schools do not necessarily teach Korean to their children at home. One parent who was interviewed is also a heritage Korean teacher. She complained of not receiving adequate support from parents to teach Korean at the Korean school:

> I feel that what I do with the kids for a few hours a week really doesn't make a difference. I try hard to get the kids to speak Korean in class but they feel so much more comfortable speaking English. Telling them to speak Korean is like pulling teeth. I don't think a lot of Korean parents really take this language thing very seriously. They just assume that sending their kids to Korean language school a few hours a week will make them fluent in Korean. And I see a lot of parents speaking English to their kids when they drop them off. How can they expect us to teach them Korean when they don't even speak it to their kids?

As for parents who do not send their children to weekend Korean schools, scheduling conflict with extracurricular activities was the number one reason (see Question 5 below). Furthermore, while some parents reported having to work on weekends and had trouble transporting children to and from school, others felt that their children have adequate conversational skills in Korean and, therefore, do not need to go to Korean schools. Other reasons include both parents' and children's lack of interest in learning Korean, often stemming from ineffective instruction and excessive homework (see also Chapter 7 for a discussion of heritage-language teacher training). Similar findings regarding lack of heritage-language school participation have been reported in other studies dealing with different immigrant communities in the US (e.g. Greek Orthodox Archdiocese of America, 1999).

Children's violent objection to speaking Korean is a significant factor in parents' decision to stop using Korean at home. One mother of two teenagers in the interview reported that her children spoke Korean very well when they were little. However, once they started going to school, they spoke English at home, which she did not think much of at first. The children spoke more and more English at home until one day, they refused to speak Korean even when she asked them to do so. She then designated two hours during the day when everyone had to speak only Korean. Much to her disappointment however, the children simply kept their mouths shut when it was 'Korean time' and resumed talking in English when it was over. She decided after trying and failing repeatedly to make them to speak Korean that it was better to have them talk in English than to have them not talk at all. She was tired of continuously 'fighting' with the children and decided to let them speak English all the time.

Keeping Korean alive is perhaps more difficult in homes where only one parent speaks it. A first-generation immigrant woman married to a second-generation Korean American in the interview reported that when her eldest daughter was born, she spoke to her exclusively in Korean out of her desire to raise her bilingually. She and her husband communicated mostly in English because he spoke very little Korean. The child entered preschool when she turned three and soon started speaking English to her mother. One day, she told her mother to stop speaking Korean and to speak to her in English like everyone else. The mother was shocked and hurt that her three-year-old daughter demanded that she stop speaking Korean to her. At first, she tried to convince her daughter that speaking Korean is a desirable attribute but that did not seem to really work. In the end, she felt tired of trying to 'swim upstream' and decided that it was much easier to simply 'let go' and switch to English, which she did.

Parents' Attitude and Behavior toward Bilingual Development

The responses to the survey showed that parental attitude and behavior toward children's English development are generally in agreement – the parents who want their children to speak English at home tend to teach and read more to their children in English (see Table 6.9). This, however, was not the case for the development of Korean, as parents who want more Korean spoken at home did not necessarily teach or read to their children in Korean. Furthermore, parents who want more Korean to be spoken at home do not necessarily send their children to weekend Korean schools. Given these findings, we may ask why there is such disparity between parents' attitude and behavior toward the development of Korean. One reason for this may be that, as mentioned earlier, the respondents own few relevant reading materials in Korean – without books in Korean, it is difficult to build literacy skills in that language. However, perhaps the bigger reason may be that in the parents' minds, Korean literacy skills have little direct relevance to children's school performance and, therefore, not requiring explicit support. Whereas the mastery of English is seen to exert immediate influence on children's success in school, acquisition and maintenance of Korean bear little urgency in the minds of many parents. This issue will be explored further in the next section.

Table 6.9 Chi-square tests of independence between respondents' desired language and their efforts toward children's language development

	Send children to Korean school	*Teach Korean to children*	*Read in Korean to children*	*Teach English to children*	*Read in English to children*
Desired home language (K, K and E, or E)	1.613	3.055	5.503	9.461[b]	23.057[c]
Desired outside language (K, K and E, or E)	4.771	4.514	5.123	1.976	8.480[a]

[a] $p<0.05$; [b] $p<0.01$; [c] $p<0.005$

Factors that Contribute to Language Shift in the Family

To raise immigrant children bilingually in a mostly monolingual society such as the United States, a great deal of effort is required to support the development of the weaker, minority languages. If parents have positive attitudes toward the development and retention of the heritage language among children, why do so many parents allow (or even encourage) their children to use English at home? In the following, I discuss some of the more major personal, social and educational pressures to shift to English in the immigrant family.

Parents' emphasis on education

In the Korean American family, language shift is accelerated in part by parents' extreme emphasis on education, which is perceived to depend largely on perfect acquisition and use of English (see also Chapter 2). Korean parents seem to be willing to support the development of bilingualism in children, so long as they feel that the use of Korean would not interfere with the acquisition and command of English. Recall from Chapter 2 that many of the Korean immigrants are well educated and have white-collar work experiences in Korea. Despite their superior educational and occupational backgrounds, however, the great majority of Korean immigrants experience downward mobility upon immigration due to their relatively low proficiency in English. Many Koreans hold marginalized jobs and work long hours as self-employed small shopkeepers. The physical and psychological stress that is generated from this downward shift makes many Korean immigrants determined to see their children excel in school, receive college and advanced degrees and enjoy brighter career prospects in mainstream America.

On the whole, the desire to see children achieve educational success in America leads many parents to approve English as the language of choice for children. Although some may have been able to achieve financial security through small businesses, very few parents would like to see their children inherit the family business. Since many see their lack of English skills as what has precluded them from participating in mainstream American society, they consider their children's fluent command of English a top priority. This is why English acquisition carries with it a great deal of urgency for parents, whereas sustained development of Korean, while exceedingly desirable, is often not of pressing importance in the hectic day-to-day schedule of immigrant family life.

Poor advice from professionals

Parents of bilingual children all over the world have routinely been advised by doctors, speech therapists, teachers and counselors to stop speaking the native language and switch to the societal language at home for the children's sake (see for example, Crepin-Lanzarotto, 1997; Schechter & Bayley, 1997). Bilingual children are more often referred to speech therapists than are monolingual children for their apparent lack of age-appropriate English skills.

One of the Korean parents in the interview, the mother of a girl seven years old, and a boy six years old, was advised by a speech therapist to speak English at home to her children. Like many Korean parents, this mother is very education-oriented and sent both of her children to preschool. When Danny turned three, he was enrolled in a local preschool in Austin, Texas, where over 90% of the student population was white. This preschool did not have an ESL program and Danny was submersed in an all-English curriculum. Several months into the semester, Danny's teacher told her that he might have some speech problems because he never talked in class. She informed her that Danny always plays by himself and does not seem to get along with other children in the class. She referred him to a speech therapist to be tested. There was also some indication that Danny might have had problems in Korean as well. The boy's paternal grandparents who lived with the family and took care of the children had been noticing that he seemed much slower in his Korean development than his older sister. She then decided that she could lose nothing by taking him to be tested by a language professional.

The speech therapist she took him to tested the boy (in English) and asked questions regarding his linguistic history. When Danny's mother shared that he seems to be slow in his development of Korean, the speech therapist advised her that children acquiring two languages tend to experience more difficulty than children who need to acquire only one. She suggested it would be better for Danny to learn one language well, and since he seems to be a slow language learner anyway, that everyone in the family start speaking only English to him. Although she was uncomfortable with the idea of discontinuing the use of Korean with her son, she felt that the advice seemed to make some sense. She reasoned that it is probably easier for Danny to learn one language than two languages. Danny's parents faithfully followed the advice of the speech therapist and started speaking only English to him. They made labels in English for common household objects and reviewed them daily with their son. They also made him repeat words and phrases in English for additional practice and read to him daily in English.

When Danny turned four, the family moved to Dallas. He was enrolled in an ESL pre-kindergarten class at a local elementary school where all of the students came from homes where languages other than English were spoken. This class, unlike his previous mainstream class, had students of Asian, Hispanic and other immigrant backgrounds who were learning English for the first time. The mother observed that the boy seemed to be far more confident and capable of expressing himself in this class, probably because he felt no different from the other children who were also trying to learn English. The teacher was also trained and certified to teach English as a second language and adapted the curriculum for young English-language learners. Danny's mother then realized that the reason why he did not talk in class the previous year was not because he had a speech problem but because he was submersed in an all English-speaking school with no help with English.

When Danny turned five, he was placed in a mainstream kindergarten class and had very little problem with his English. He was now very talkative and played with his classmates well. The family continued to speak exclusively English. Danny is now seven years old and is a fluent English speaker. One day, his maternal grandparents visited the family from out of town and were shocked that he could speak no Korean. The grandparents suggested to the parents that they start teaching him Korean again before it was too late. The parents were now worried that he would not be able to speak Korean at all and have hired a Korean tutor. It is not clear how much success Danny would have in re-learning Korean since he goes to an English-medium school and his Korean instruction is limited to only a few hours a week. The parents have now started to speak Korean to him again but whenever he is prompted to speak in Korean, he either says nothing or responds in English. Since he does not even understand simple utterances in Korean, the parents often end up switching to English when addressing him.

Since sufficient data on Danny's language use and socialization at home and in school are not available, it is difficult to determine exactly what combination of factors may have contributed to the initial delay in his speech. What is clear, however, is that he has lost several critical years in early childhood to stabilize his fragile knowledge of Korean to handle the inevitable encounter with English later. With the presence of English all around him, he now has much fewer chances to use and practice Korean in meaningful ways. From Danny's point of view, Korean is now much more difficult to speak correctly than is English and may not be worth the enormous effort. Had his Korean had more time to develop without the overwhelming influence of English, he is likely to have learned to speak Korean quite well, as he speaks English fluently now. While he may have been slower in his speech development than the average child, he apparently did not have any particular language disability.

What is unfortunate about this and other similar cases is that bilingualism is often believed to be the cause of language problems in linguistic minority children. Many parents and teachers believe that children will be confused with input from two languages and experience slower and incomplete cognitive development, leading to academic failure (see also Chapter

1 for a discussion of 'semilingualism'). However, the argument that bilingual input confuses children is not valid since most children growing up in bilingual or multilingual societies acquire two or more languages with no apparent negative consequences to their cognitive development. Korean parents are anxious to see their children excel academically even at very early ages. The possibility that their children may fall behind in school is a genuine source of worry. As this case illustrates, parents are extremely vulnerable to the advice of teachers and childcare professionals who presumably know what is best for the children.

The assessment of language minority children should take a multifaceted approach. At the minimum, the assessment should take both of the child's languages into account. A realistic assessment of bilingual children must be based firmly on knowledge of developmental norms for the two languages, typical patterns of language transference and patterns of socialization both within and outside the family (Cummins, 1996). However, since there is currently no general agreement among child language researchers about the 'normal' course of development among monolingual, let alone, bilingual children, this issue is not so straightforward (Romaine, 1995). The wide range of individual differences in language acquisition and patterns of exposure to bilingual input make the determination of 'normal' bilingual development an elusive concept. Nonetheless, advising parents to abandon the native language hurts children and their families in very profound ways.

Policies that favor English-only

Aside from poor advice from professionals, there are greater societal forces that drive parents to switch to English. In Chapter 1, I discussed that reinforcing immigrant children's native languages in early childhood and early grades of elementary school and delaying the introduction of English until later grades is, in fact, an important component of successful bilingual education programs for language minority children. I also discussed that strong support of immigrant children's first languages throughout schooling contributes significantly to academic success. Given that the research on enrichment bilingual education programs has consistently shown the advantages of developing and maintaining students' first languages, why do most bilingual programs in the United States continue to be transitional? The answer to this question lies in a social context that explicitly devalues ethnic languages.

Although the official policy toward linguistic minorities has been neither one of encouragement nor one of repression but more a policy of toleration in the US, the general attitude of the Anglo-American majority has been that members of linguistic minorities should integrate themselves into the English-speaking society as quickly as possible (Grosjean, 1982). Americans believe that the maintenance of ethnic languages and culture should be tolerated but they should not slow down the acquisition of English and the rapid assimilation of the immigrant into American life. Efforts to make English the only language in governments, hospital and schools have been on the rise in the US (see e.g. Macedo, 2000; Shannon, 1999). During the 1980s and 1990s, the 'US English' organization coordinated much of the opposition to bilingual education, initiating and passing referenda in more than 20 states to make English the official language (Cazden & Snow, 1990; Crawford, 1992). These measures make the use of languages other than English illegal in governmental and educational domains. This means that minority languages cannot be used to register voters or educate children of minority backgrounds in those languages, which effectively reduces the amount of participation in American government by minority populations.

In recent years, there have been changes in educational policy, both at the state and federal levels, which have placed language minority children at a distinct disadvantage. For example, voters in California (1998) and Arizona (2000), and, most recently, in Massachusetts (2002) passed initiatives to replace most bilingual programs with all-English immersion programs that are intended to last only one year. Given that it takes anywhere between four and seven years to develop academic English skills (see also Cummins, 1996; Ramirez, 1992), the one-year standard of English acquisition is unrealistic and will have a disproportionate, adverse effect on poor children, by arbitrarily terminating language services on which they are most dependent (Crawford, 2000). The organization 'English for the Children', which campaigned for English-only education in these states claim that bilingual education hurts children and immersion in English is the solution to low-performing immigrant children (Crawford, 1992). They claim that bilingual education programs teach children too little English and rob them of the opportunity to be mainstreamed. They blame the educational failure of Hispanic students, who have the highest dropout rates among minority groups, on bilingual education.

In addition, the current efforts for national educational reform, which stress regular testing of all students to keep schools accountable, are particularly hurting language minority children. High school exit examinations that test English, math and reasoning skills in English have now been adopted by 30 states and students who do not pass these tests leave high school with a 'certificate of attendance' rather than a high school diploma, even if they have taken and passed all required coursework (Wong

Fillmore, 2003). These do the greatest harm to immigrant students who arrive in the United States in their secondary school years since many of them will not have fully acquired academic English proficiency by the time they are ready to graduate from high school.

Most recently, the reauthorized Elementary and Secondary Education Act (ESEA), subtitled 'No Child Left Behind Act' (NCLBA) (2002) mandates assessments of English proficiency for limited English proficient (LEP) students each year and achievement testing in English for students that have been in US schools for at least three years (Crawford, n.d.). This legislation has the goal of quickly moving language minority students into mainstream classes and pays no attention to helping students develop and maintain their first languages. Instead, a rapid transition into English-only instruction will take precedence and states must set 'annual measurable achievement objectives' for schools to move LEP students toward English proficiency and to help them meet high standards. Under this legislation, all references to promoting bilingualism in language minority children have been removed from what used to be called the Bilingual Education Act (1968). Even the word 'bilingual' is deleted from what was once the Federal Office of Bilingual Education and Minority Languages Affairs (OBEMLA), now renamed as the Office of English Language Acquisition, Language Enhancement, and Academic Achievement for Limited English Proficient Students (OELA). Benchmarks for program evaluations will include the percentage of students reclassified as fluent in English each year and 'adequate yearly progress' on English-language achievement tests. Schools that fall short of these objectives face penalty in the form of restructuring and/or discontinued funding.

Teachers are, therefore, pressured to abandon any existing support for developing students' home languages and to focus solely on helping students develop their English skills. The odds are very much against immigrant parents who would like to pass down the mother tongue to their children. Parents and students are choosing English only programs out of a fear that any use of the children's native language at school will delay the mastery of English (Wong Fillmore, 2003). This certainly is true for many Korean immigrant parents who spend great sums of money on extra help for their children's academic work in English. When presented with a choice between English only and increased chance for success in school, on the one hand, and bilingualism and failure in school, on the other, parents undoubtedly would choose the former.

Summary

In this chapter, I discussed personal, social and educational factors that contribute to language shift in the Korean American family and community. Results of the questionnaire suggest that language shift within the Korean American family is well under way, lending support to Fishman's (1989: 206) observation that 'what begins as the language of social and economic mobility ends, within three generations or so, as the language of the crib as well, even in democratic and pluralism-permitting contexts.' In general, the extent of language shift in the Korean American family is strongly related to the degree of the respondents' exposure to English. More specifically, length of residence in the United States was a strong predictor of parental language use and attitude. As length of residence increased, the respondents became generally more proficient in English, were more approving of children speaking English at home, taught and read more English to their children and assumed a more American identity than those with shorter US residence. Respondents' age at immigration was also a strong indicator of language shift, which suggests that with increasing years of exposure to English, parents' comfort levels with English also increase, resulting in greater use and acceptance of English in daily life.

In general, the parents reported relatively low proficiency in English despite remarkably high levels of education and urban white-collar work experiences in Korea. This has led the great majority of Korean immigrants to experience downward mobility as a consequence of immigration, holding marginalized jobs or working long hours as self-employed small shopkeepers (Hurh, 1998). While many parents recognize the intrinsic linguistic and cultural value of maintaining Korean, they also see their lack of English skills as constraining their participation in the wider American society, limiting their opportunity to be included on an equal footing with mainstream Americans. Many first generation parents are, therefore, determined to see their children develop strong English skills and provide explicit support for children's acquisition of English literacy. However, parents who want Korean to be spoken at home do not necessarily read to their children in Korean nor send them to weekend Korean schools. Although most parents would like their children to use and maintain Korean, a fluent command of English is certainly a higher priority.

Immigrant parents may *choose* to shift to English for a variety of reasons. One of the reasons is parents' perception that English is critical for academic and social success in America. This is similar in some respects to the phenomenon described by Kamwangamalu (2003), who explains the social and political changes that have occurred in South Africa since 1994 that have led to politically supported indigenous languages of numerically large groups being voluntarily 'surrendered' so that children can acquire English, the economically dominant language that was for so many years the object of restricted teaching and acquisition. English acquisition is surely perceived as a prized asset, a key to opening doors and a road to better opportunities. Parents also aspire to become bilingual themselves as the attainment of unaccented, fluent English is often equated with prestige in the Korean American community.

I also discussed the consequences of advice given to parents by well-meaning but ill-informed teachers, doctors and speech therapists to stop speaking the native language to children at home. The effects of English-only policies on the education of language minority children and how immigrant children are particularly hurt by the current national frenzy over testing and evaluation of all students was also touched upon. In sum, the pressures for language minority individuals and families to abandon their native languages are without doubt enormous. Although recently there seems to be a resurgence of interest in mother-tongue maintenance, practical elements to support mother-tongue development, such as well-trained Korean teachers and high-quality textbooks and materials in Korean are in considerably short supply. Lack of tangible support for mother-tongue maintenance at both the familial and institutional levels is likely to speed up the pace of language shift in the Korean American community (Fishman 1989), as evidenced in many second-generation Korean American homes where mostly English is spoken.

However, this does not mean that heritage languages cannot be transmitted and maintained. In the next chapter, I make suggestions for successful transfer and maintenance of heritage languages.

Chapter 7

Developing and Maintaining Heritage Languages

In this chapter, I discuss the major findings from the previous chapters and provide suggestions for successfully developing and maintaining minority languages.

This book attempted to show that bilingualism in linguistic minority children is a resource to be nurtured and promoted, not a problem to be solved. Rather than looking at immigrant children as being deficient in English, this book argued that one needs to consider children's native languages as an additional asset. Along this line, I examined codeswitching, which is an integral component of bilingual conversation. There is a great deal of negative perception about codeswitching – monolinguals and bilinguals alike often view codeswitching as a lazy, haphazard mixture of two languages. People commonly think that those who codeswitch know neither language well enough to converse in one language only. Teachers often frown upon students who codeswitch in the classroom and think that it is evidence of some sort of linguistic deficiency in bilingual children. Contrary to all of these beliefs, however, we have seen that language mixing is a natural conversational phenomenon, used strategically to convey various social and rhetorical meanings to other participants in the conversation.

I have analyzed different instances of codeswitching as either participant-related or discourse-related. Specifically, the analysis of participant-related codeswitching showed that the Korean–English bilingual children use codeswitching as a result of personal preference for and competence in one language or the other and to negotiate the language for the interaction. As the conversation proceeds, the children carefully observe their partner's speech production and adapt their own language choice to their assessment of the bilingual abilities and preferences of the other participants. In terms of discourse-related codeswitching, I showed that the Korean–English bilingual children use codeswitching as a general conversational strategy to structure their discourse. Overall, the sequential analysis suggested that codeswitching is used as an *additional* means to communicate the speaker's intents and preferences to other participants in the conversation. This conclusion directly questions the assumption that codeswitching is evidence of communicative deficit in bilingual children.

Although codeswitching is used as an interactive tool, it was found in only a very small portion of the overall speech data collected in the mainstream classroom. The fact that codeswitching is so rare was argued to be an additional motivation for explaining its use as an interactive resource in pragmatic terms. In general, the young Korean American children seem to have a clear understanding that they are expected to use English in the classroom. Five of the 12 children particularly preferred English, which was usually accommodated by their Korean peers who switched to English despite their own preference for Korean. Conversations in which each child spoke a different language (i.e. one child speaking only English and the other speaking only Korean) almost always resulted in the Korean-speaking child switching to English and the children conducting the rest of the conversation in that language. Thus, the children's codeswitching patterns were reflective of the uneven distribution of power represented by the two languages and the children's socialization into the cultural norms of mainstream American classrooms which discourage the use of languages other than English.

In addition to codeswitching, I examined two specific aspects of the Korean children's language acquisition, as related to their bilingual interaction. First, the morpheme study sought to examine how child L2 learners of English learn English grammatical features, examining specifically the role of L1 structures on L2 acquisition. Comparison of rank orders of acquisition of ten English morphemes by different L2 learner groups (including the Korean children) suggested that the structure of the learner's L1 influences the sequence of acquisition of L2 grammatical features. Given the high degree of similarity in grammatical structures in Korean and Japanese and given the high level of correlation in the rank order of acquisition of English morphemes by Korean and Japanese children, it was suggested that acquisition of L2 grammatical categories is influenced by the grammatical categories in the learner's first language.

Among the ten English morphemes, the bilingual Korean children experienced particular difficulty with the indefinite article, the third person singular -s and the plural morpheme. But it was the English plural morpheme, which presented the greatest difficulty to the Korean children, and, therefore, this was examined in greater detail in the experimental study. The experimental study sought to investigate ways in which the bilingual Korean American children handle the different plural-marking systems of English and Korean. It revealed that at least in terms of acquisition of plural marking, the Korean American children temporarily lag behind monolinguals of either language. Since bilingual children use the two languages in different circumstances with different people and since the children were exposed to English later in childhood, it is perhaps not surprising that they do not exhibit the same level of acquisitional maturity in either language as do monolingual children. Just as errors are a natural part of L1 acquisition, L2 acquisition is expected to entail periods of error-ridden productions. The fact that the children's L1 is still in the process of being learned adds an additional layer of complexity to the dynamic nature of their bilingual language development. It is important to remember that the children are constantly in the process of developing in the two languages and that their bilingualism is never a static entity.

It remains to be seen how the current pattern of delayed grammatical acquisition will change in the course of the children's development. Nonetheless, based on most available accounts of Korean American children, it is expected that the children's current errors in English will disappear as they become more and more proficient in English. The children's Korean however, is likely to weaken progressively given the subtractive school environment that discourages the use of minority languages. With so much emphasis on the acquisition of English, all of the 12 Korean American children will be mainstreamed as soon as they are deemed adequately proficient to handle instruction in English. Once mainstreamed, even the little Korean they used to hear in the transitional bilingual pull-out class will no longer be available. Without systematic and persistent effort to maintain Korean at the family and community level, the majority of the children are likely eventually to lose Korean.

The observation that bilingual children temporarily lag behind monolingual children in grammatical development in both languages can be easily misinterpreted to mean that bilingualism hurts children. Opponents of bilingual education argue that it is better for children to be exposed to one language and learn it well than to be burdened with two and learn neither one completely. Minority children are, therefore, advised to learn the language of the school and stop using the native language. Many parents and teachers also believe that discontinuing the use of the native language will help children learn English better and more quickly. However, a great deal of research shows that English immersion does not necessarily make children more fluent in English or acquire it more quickly. In fact, there is evidence that premature mainstreaming of linguistic minority children into English-only classes hurts their academic performance as they fall progressively further behind (Crawford, 2000; Cummins, 1996). However, the idea that English acquisition takes at least several years is not very welcomed by anxious parents who are terrified at the thought that their children might do poorly in school even for a short period of time. Parents as well as teachers and school policy-makers usually demand quick results and this is probably why, regardless of what research says, people continually make decisions based on their intuitions, which unfortunately are based on myths rather than facts.

Bilingualism is an elusive concept for language minority populations. Although immigrants desire to be bilingual in both their native language and the language of the host society, they experience enormous pressures to choose one or the other (and often ending up with neither), as Hornberger (1998: 446) aptly points out:

> ... the plea of immigrants is that they ought to be enabled to learn and use the new language, but also to keep and use their own language, the 'old' language, in their new country. This twin plea, an expression of immigrant bilingual versatility, is remarkably consistent around the world; yet what is equally remarkable and consistent around the world is that the immigrants' new country often seeks to force a choice for one or the other language – or worse still, ignores both pleas.

Immigrant parents know all too well that a fluent command of English is a requirement for success in American schools and society. Despite their relatively high levels of education and professional training, many Korean immigrants experience difficulty finding professional jobs due to their lack of English skills. Many Korean immigrants end up working in self-owned small businesses, which, on the one hand, do not require high levels of English proficiency but which on the other hand, are lower in social status than professional jobs. In status-conscious Korean American society, lack of competence in English is, therefore, equated with lower social status. Because they find English so difficult to master, Korean parents are determined to see that their children become fully competent in English and enjoy better career opportunities. Parents often praise their children for speaking English well, which has the effect of subtly reinforcing the idea that English is the more important language.

While immigrant parents know the practical value of knowing English well, they would also like their children to maintain the native language. In fact, the vast majority of the parents surveyed have a negative attitude toward Koreans living in America who cannot speak Korean. For most Korean parents, proficiency in Korean is a marker of social identity and what distinguishes Korean Americans from other ethnic groups in America. Although Korean does not carry with it an urgent practical need for life in the USA as English does, parents consider it critical for intergenerational communication and participation in the Korean ethnic community. However, since it is not directly tied to school performance, on which parents place huge emphasis, Korean does not enjoy the kind of explicit support that English receives. Many Korean parents hire private tutors or send their children to after-school tutoring academies to provide them with extra help with schoolwork in English but rarely do they hire tutors to teach children Korean. Therefore, one practical way to support the maintenance of Korean would be to integrate it more centrally into the regular school curriculum (see suggestions for heritage-language maintenance provided later in this chapter).

When it comes to minority-language maintenance, parental attitude and behavior often do not go hand in hand – while parents may have a positive attitude toward children's maintenance of the heritage language, it does not always translate to actual support for the development of the mother tongue. I have already discussed that lack of knowledge about bilingualism leads to parental disapproval of dual-language education as a viable alternative for children's education in America. Language minority parents are swayed by public opinion that bilingualism retards children's cognitive and linguistic development. In an attempt to spare them of the potential academic difficulties they are thought to encounter in school, parents may enroll their children in English-only classes. However, parents may also be forced to choose English-only instruction because the bilingual alternatives are simply of poor quality. Inadequately trained teachers and poorly planned curriculum and instruction are sufficient reasons for parents to avoid enrolling their children in ESL or bilingual education programs. Since the education of language minority students is a low priority in many school districts in the United States, ESL and bilingual education often receive limited funding and are relegated to marginal, if not stigmatized, status. Instead of given the option of acquiring English while maintaining the mother tongue, immigrants are almost always presented with a choice of one or the other, often resulting in the majority language being learned at the expense of the native language.

In a social context that systematically devalues ethnic languages and cultures, parents and teachers alike are under enormous social pressures to abandon work on children's native languages. English-only educational policies and high-stakes testing are particularly damaging to language minority students because they give no regard to the linguistic and cultural resources children bring to school. What are the costs associated with educating language minority children in English only? Grosjean (1982: 212–3) sums it up well in the following quote:

I must stress once again that educating the minority child in the majority language can have many problems. Admittedly, many children do make it through the system, but at what cost! They often lose their native language and culture in the process. Many turn their backs on their minority group (they have gone 'up and out') and assimilate themselves into the majority, often becoming the strongest proponents of the argument, 'I made it through, why can't you?' But many other children are left by the wayside: they have fallen behind in school, have failed to master the majority language well, feel insecure, and often have negative attitudes toward both the majority group that rejects them and the minority group they have been taught to look down upon. It is in this sense that monolingual education is too costly.

Although a great deal of research on enrichment bilingual education programs has consistently shown the advantages of developing and maintaining students' first languages, most schools in the United States continue to operate on the basis of English-only policies. In such context, what can be done to transmit and maintain minority languages successfully? Here I provide some practical suggestions for parents, schools and communities.

Intergenerational Transmission of Heritage Languages

Since each linguistic minority community is different, different sets of solutions for language maintenance are required for different communities. However, successful language-maintenance strategies usually involve the initiative of the linguistic minority communities that provide the impetus for language-planning efforts which must start with intergenerational language transmission at the level of the family (Fishman, 1991; Hornberger, 1998). Fishman (1991: xii) states that to attempt to maintain a minority language through efforts to control the language of education, the workplace, the mass media and governmental services, without having sufficiently protected the intergenerational transmission of heritage language is like 'constantly blowing air into a tire that still has a puncture'. In order for minority languages to thrive, they must first be learned, used and enjoyed by young people. Communities where young people no longer acquire the native language are in great danger of completely shifting to the dominant language. Since it is impossible to maintain what is not transmitted in the first place, protecting the minority language at home is of vital importance. In order to pass on the heritage languages to children, parents need to do at least the following:

- Speak the heritage language (HL) at home and insist that children respond in that language.
- Encourage children to speak the HL and do not criticize incorrect grammar or pronunciation. Teach older children to encourage younger siblings' attempts to speak the HL and to not ridicule incorrect productions (Shin, 2002a).
- Emphasize the value of learning the HL and instill pride in the heritage language and culture.
- Acquire age-appropriate HL reading materials and TV programs that are interesting and comprehensible to children.
- Read often to children in the HL.
- Teach children how to read and write the HL.
- Send children to heritage language schools and be actively involved in children's HL education.
- Provide opportunities for children to use the HL in meaningful contexts with peers who value the HL.
- Take children on trips to the country of origin.

In general, parents should insist that their children address them in the HL and resist the temptation to respond in English. Children who grow up proficient in both the HL and the socially dominant language often come from homes where the HL was spoken as a matter of policy (Bayley *et al.* 1996; Cho & Krashen, 2000; Hakuta & D'Andrea, 1992; Kondo, 1998; Portes & Hao, 1998). Bayley *et al.*, (1996) suggest that a 'household ban' on English helped ensure children's development of Spanish in one Mexican American family. Parental use of the HL is crucial in children's development of their native languages.

Parents should also seek to maintain a diverse collection of books and print materials in the HL and read them to children often. This helps to elevate the status of the HL in the minds of immigrant children and helps them develop positive attitudes toward L1 literacy. As discussed in Chapter 6, lack of appropriate reading materials in the HL is a pervasive problem in many language minority homes. Since HL books tend to be more difficult to locate and generally more expensive than books written in English, community organizations and local libraries can assist in acquiring and circulating HL books to the wider community. Parents should also read in the HL themselves and show children that reading in the HL can be enjoyable and worthwhile. Whenever possible, trips to the country of origin may provide children with additional opportunities to use the HL in meaningful contexts. In addition, parents should carefully choose a quality HL program and be actively involved in the school.

Heritage Language Education

What is the role of heritage schools in minority language maintenance? Tse (1998b) reviews available studies comparing ethnic minority students who have exposure to HL programs and others who do not. She concludes that HL programs have a positive impact on language attitudes in most studies, suggesting beneficial outcomes from exposure to and/or instruction in the language. The subjects reported greater appreciation of the HL, confidence in using it, enjoyment in doing schoolwork in the language, and a desire to continue learning it. In addition, exposure to HL programs promotes a positive association and closer identification with one's own ethnic group. In addition, all of the successful HL speakers in Tse's (2001) study had enjoyed the institutional support provided by school approval of the HL, either in the community or through their mainstream schools. The positive experiences primarily centered around experiences where teachers and/or classmates valued the language ability the participants brought with them from home. For example, one student with a Mexican background realized the usefulness of knowing Spanish when he enrolled in Spanish courses in high school and the other students vied for his help on assignments.

In another study of a group of US native bilinguals who have managed to develop high levels of literacy in both English and their HL, Tse (2001) found that each participant saw their HL as being highly vital (useful and even prestigious) and had (1) a peer group that used the HL; (2) contact with institutions that valued the language; and (3) parents who spoke the HL and encouraged its development. Among these, having a peer group who values the HL was the most critical. At some point in their lives, each participant became part of a peer group who valued the HL. Possessing HL ability was critical for gaining access to, getting full membership in and/or achieving a prominent position within the particular social group. A second base of support that boosted the participants' opinions of the HL came from formal institutions that valued HL proficiency. In all of the cases, learning the HL began with exposure to language and literacy experiences in the home and community at an early age. For all of the participants, this linguistic foundation was available through adolescence and early adulthood, when proficiency in the language became more important for school, career, and/or identity development.

Although school participation in HL maintenance has many benefits, the conditions in which HLs are taught are not always optimal. In the next section, I describe the current state of Korean HL education in America and offer suggestions for effective HL instruction in schools.

Korean schools

There are currently over one thousand Korean HL schools in the United States, most of which are organized and operated by Korean Christian churches. Many of these programs are small and offer a limited selection of courses. One of the major concerns of these programs is a lack of texts that are written specifically for heritage learners of Korean. Much of the instructional materials that are currently used in Korean HL schools in America have been 'donated from Korean embassies and have been formatted for Korean learning styles and lifestyles that are foreign to Korean American children' (Lee, 2002). There is also a general shortage of age-appropriate texts for older beginners (i.e. secondary school students and adults), who are put off by the childish content in many beginning Korean texts. Books written for second-generation Korean Americans about Korean culture and history and the Korean immigrant experience are also very much in need (but see National Association for Korean Schools, 2002).

Another major concern of Korean heritage schools is teacher development. Due to limited resources, teachers are usually paid minimally and receive little adequate professional training. Many programs suffer from a high teacher turnover rate, which adds to the problem of staff development and training. Most teachers in Korean HL schools have been educated in Korea and teach in the way in which they have been taught – a great deal of instructional time is spent on rote learning, drills and memorization. As a result, most heritage learners, who are accustomed to an instructional method that encourages student participation and creative thinking, find much of the instruction in Korean schools tedious and unproductive. Korean-educated teachers and American-educated students hold different expectations of what constitutes acceptable student behavior in the classroom. For example, Korean-educated teachers see themselves as primary transmitters of knowledge and expect students passively to absorb materials taught in a largely lecture-style manner. Few teachers are familiar with techniques for eliciting student input and organizing and supervising group activities, which are especially important in language classrooms. Teachers may also feel threatened by students who ask too many questions.

The collision of learning and teaching styles in the HL classroom calls for a teacher recruiting strategy that specifically targets the so-called '1.5-generation' Korean Americans. These are individuals who have the bilingual and bicultural capacity to 'go between' the Korean-speaking first generation and the English-speaking second generation. Most 1.5-generationers were born in Korea and came to the United States during school age and have been educated in both countries. Since they are familiar with both styles of teaching and have first-hand experience in cultural adaptation,

1.5-generationers can provide useful insights to the development of curriculum materials that are geared specifically for second-generation Korean Americans. Since they are bilingual, they can explain grammatical concepts in English and act as cultural mediators between parents and children. Of course, 1.5-generation teachers should be supported to further develop their literacy skills in Korean and trained in effective language teaching methods. One promising option for heritage teacher development is a three-way model in which first-generation teachers and 1.5-generation teachers work collaboratively with university-level teacher-training programs. This type of model enables the provision of professional development that is specifically tailored to meet the needs of both groups of heritage teachers who may or may not be English speaking. Teachers may learn about student-centered, theme-based language-teaching methods that raise awareness of language use as well as classroom management techniques (see also Schwartz, 2001).

Korean as a foreign language subject

Korean is currently offered as a foreign language in public schools in certain districts with high concentrations of Korean populations (e.g. Fairfax County, Virginia, New York City). For the first time, in 1997, Korean was included as one of the SAT II elective subjects, which assess students' knowledge of a particular subject for college admission. This has stimulated interest and motivation for learning Korean among young Korean Americans and their parents (Lee, 2002). Hurh (1998) reports that there are more than 25 Korean schools in the Chicago area which offer intensive courses in the Korean language and culture for students preparing to take the SAT II in Korean. Short of a full integration of Korean into the school curriculum, these measures serve as first steps in successfully developing and maintaining Korean because they recognize Korean as a legitimate academic subject. It is, therefore, not surprising that there is currently a great deal of interest in taking Korean as a foreign-language subject among Korean Americans. For example, 85% of the Korean American undergraduate and graduate students in Lee's (2002) survey indicated that they would have enrolled in a Korean class if it had been offered in their primary or secondary school. Given Korean parents' emphasis on education, the more Korean is integrated into the regular school curriculum, the more likely it will be valued and learned.

Since there is evidence that negative feelings toward the ethnic culture and HL prevents the HL from being learned (Tse, 1998a), there must be a concerted effort on the part of the school, the local and Korean American communities to cultivate positive feelings toward the Korean language and culture. Needless to say, in order for Korean to be perceived as positive and valuable, its curriculum and instruction need to be interesting, effective and exerting a positive influence over the lives of its users. Proficiency in Korean should be seen as valuable not only by Korean children but also by children of other backgrounds. It should not be relegated to a lower status, as has traditionally been the case for bilingual education, but it should be seen as equal in status to the other foreign languages that are offered at the school. There also needs to be cooperation among HL schools, public schools, local communities and universities in terms of professional development for teachers and staff, a pooling of resources (e.g. books and other educational materials in Korean) and for organizing and operating programs.

Korean–English dual language programs

Other than offering Korean as a foreign-language subject, a more effective solution for maintaining Korean is to integrate it more fully into the regular school-day curriculum (see also Feuerverger, 1989; Tse, 2001). Examples of this can be found in dual language programs that follow an enrichment bilingual education model. There are currently six two-way Korean–English immersion programs (two elementary schools and two middle schools) in California (Center for Applied Linguistics, n.d.; Kim, 2003). The Center for Applied Linguistics defines two-way immersion programs as those in which

(1) language-minority and language-majority students are integrated for at least 50% of instructional time at all grade levels,
(2) the content and literacy instruction in both languages is provided to all students and
(3) there is a balance of language-minority and language-majority students, with each group making up between one-third and two-thirds of the total student population.

In the Korean–English dual-language programs, Korean and English are used separately in instruction and there is intensive staff development in areas of theory, practice and language. All of the Korean–English dual-language programs receive support in teacher training and technical assistance from the school district and university partners.

One of the frequently encountered problems in starting a dual-language program is recruiting young native English-speaking students and retaining them through subsequent grades. The Korean–English dual-language programs report organizing meetings with school staff and administrators to introduce the program to neighborhood parents, with the help of community organizations. Although recruitment was a challenge in the beginning, these programs have, over the years, established a reputation for educating highly capable students who are literate in both languages. For example, Cahuenga Elementary School, located in Koreatown in Los Angeles and home to one of the Korean–English dual language programs has been designated a School of Excellence by the California State Department of Education. This school shares the challenges facing most schools in Los Angeles United School District (LAUSD) with over 80% of students being classified as low income and of limited English proficiency. However, all students in the two-way immersion program read and write in both English and Korean. Students in the program outperform their LAUSD peers in English-only programs on Stanford 9 and CTBS-U standardized tests in English reading, language and math. This has helped to boost the status of Korean in the eyes of both children and their parents. Convincing both minority- and majority-language parents of the effectiveness and benefits of dual-language instruction is the key to success in this type of enrichment and maintenance-oriented program. In addition, raising public awareness about the benefits of dual-language education, cultivating broad-based support from government, universities and the community and improving curriculum and materials are requirements for successful two-way immersion and other programs involving minority languages (Compton, 2001).

Suggestions for HL programs

Much of what we know about effective second- and foreign-language learning and teaching practices applies to HL programs, which should do at least the following:

- Provide cognitively challenging instruction that encourages active language use to connect input with students' prior experience and with thematically-related content (Chamot *et al.*, 1996; Cummins, 1996).
- Create comfortable learning environments where students are given opportunities to use the HL in situations they consider useful but are not required to do so until ready (Tse, 2001).
- Avoid overemphasis on the grammatical accuracy of student speech or writing.
- Acknowledge and value dialectal variations (Jo, 2001; Tse, 2001).
- Provide continuous professional development for teachers and staff to give HL teachers a sense of their professional identity and importance (Compton, 2001; Feuerverger, 1997)

- Form partnerships between HL teachers and regular teachers (Feuerverger, 1997).
- Form partnerships with parents and local community (Compton, 2001; Corson, 2001).
- Teach heritage cultures along with HLs (Feueverger, 1997).
- Educate teachers about the facts and myths of bilingualism and bilingual education.

One of the distinguishing features of successful indigenous language maintenance programs is close partnership with parents and local community (Christian & Genesee, 2001; Corson, 2001). One form of partnership may involve educating parents and teachers about the facts and myths of bilingualism and bilingual education. These programs can inform parents of the advantages of bilingualism but also warn them of the effort required to raise children bilingually in a monolingual society. Parents should be warned of the long-term consequences of children's loss of the mother tongue and asked to weigh the advantages and disadvantages of early exposure to English through English-speaking preschool programs. Parents and teachers should be warned that English immersion does not necessarily make children acquire English more quickly and that premature mainstreaming can have negative effects. Parental seminars may include lessons on how to read to children to increase comprehension and ways in which to secure reading materials in Korean. There should be community-wide efforts to make the HL more desirable. There is also the need for more school- and community-based research that shows the benefits of HL maintenance and dissemination of such results to HL communities and beyond.

The next section offers suggestions for mainstream teachers and schools that work with language minority children.

Suggestions for system-wide policy and practice

Despite the positive impact of HL programs, Fishman (1991: 371) notes that 'without considerable and repeated societal reinforcement', long-term HL development is unlikely. Only when bilingualism and HL proficiency are appreciated and respected by mainstream culture will HL development prevail and not require special efforts to maintain. As a nation, we need competence in languages other than English to become 'a language competent society', in Tucker's (1991) phrase. Valuing the student's first language is naturally one of the most critical steps to empowering language minority students. At the school level, all teachers (mainstream, special education, ESL) should be trained to teach language minority students.

Language minority students need to see teachers who appreciate the cultural and linguistic knowledge that they bring from home. While the student population in American schools has become increasingly diverse, the teacher population has remained overwhelmingly white. Over 90% of US public school teachers in 1996 were white (National Center for Education Statistics, n.d.). The population of Asian American school-children has doubled in recent decades, yet most make it from kindergarten through high school without ever having a teacher of their own race (Perlstein, 2000). Asians are under-represented in teaching nationwide but, in some school districts, the gaps are more pronounced. For example, in Fairfax County public schools in Virginia, 15% of the student population is Asian, as compared to 2% Asian in the faculty (Perlstein, 2000). It is difficult for language- and ethnic-minority students to have positive perceptions about their own language and culture if they never see a teacher who comes from similar background. In order to achieve a more diverse teaching population, there needs to be a concerted effort on the part of local and state educational agencies and ethnic communities to recruit teachers from language minority communities.

In general, teachers should have high expectations for all children regardless of their linguistic and cultural backgrounds and celebrate the diversity of languages and cultures in their classrooms, making it a learning experience for all students (see also Corson, 2001: 148-150). Teachers should sometimes allow students to bring books in their native language to read in school or to display materials in the native language on classroom walls. Teachers may also learn some simple expressions in the L1s of their students and prepare lessons around multicultural literature involving characters and stories from the students' backgrounds (see also Baker, 2000). It is clear that English is a language of crucial importance in the United States. The issue in the education of language minority students in America is not whether English will be taught and learned but rather when and how it should be introduced. Of course, beginning schooling in the mother tongue helps children to transition from their L1 to English.

The Road to Bilingualism

While the route children take to bilingualism is relatively straightforward and uncomplicated in bilingual or multilingual communities where most children normally acquire two, three or even more languages naturally, parents trying to raise their children bilingually in largely monolingual communities (e.g. United States, Australia) face a bigger challenge. Certainly, a positive attitude toward language maintenance is important but this alone is not sufficient to produce functional bilinguals.

Baker (2000: 62) likens the process of raising children bilingually to that of gardening:

> It is not like scattering a few seeds on the ground and expecting swift, strong and simple growth. The tender language shoots need to be nourished, the garden well fertilized in order for later blossoming and color to occur. As the seasons of language development change, the parent has constantly to tend the language garden... Just as the hard work of digging, manuring and weeding in the garden eventually produce beautiful blossoms, so with the language garden.

Raising children bilingually is hard work but the hope of seeing them develop into confident, competent multicultural citizens who are proud of their heritage and are respectful of other cultures and peoples is what makes every language maintenance effort worthwhile. Obviously, without the kind of 'considerable and repeated societal reinforcement' of HLs that Fishman (1991:371) refers to, it will be difficult to maintain minority languages. However, the more parents, communities and educators are made aware of the processes of bilingual development and convinced of the tremendous resources that linguistic minority children bring to our schools and society, the more likely it is that real change will take place. This book certainly has been an attempt to contribute to that process.

Notes

1. But see Tse (1996) and Valdés (2003) for discussions on the positive effects of language brokering on immigrant children (e.g. maturity and independence).
2. See Valadez *et al.* (2000) for a discussion of the serious problems associated with the 'semilingual' concept.
3. In this book, I use the Yale System of Romanization (see Appendix 3) for utterances in Korean (Martin, 1992).
4. In comparing subjects' success rate in correctly supplying a morpheme in an obligatory context, they measured accuracy of use, which was assumed to reflect order of acquisition.
5. For an authoritative summary of Korean history with an extensive annotated bibliography, see Choe (1980).
6. The Immigration and Naturalization Act of 1965 set an annual limit of 120,000 immigrants from the Western Hemisphere (includes South and North America and the Caribbean) and 170,000 from the Eastern Hemisphere (includes all other continents and islands), with a maximum of 20,000 for any individual country, exclusive of any immediate relatives of American citizens.
7. All names of persons, schools and places are pseudonyms.
8. The three studies that are subsequently compared with the current study (i.e. Brown, 1973; Dulay & Burt, 1974; and Hakuta, 1976) combine indefinite and definite tokens in their scoring. To facilitate comparability, these two types are merged in the scoring of the Korean children's data.
9. There were two separate categories for the plural in Dulay and Burt (1974): (1) 'short plurals' –/s/ and /z/ allomorphs – and (2) 'long plurals' – /Iz/ allomorph – as in 'churches'. However, there were only a handful of long plurals in the Korean children's data that a fair comparison with short plurals could not be made. Therefore, the long plurals in the current data were excluded so that only the short plurals can later be compared with the short plurals in Dulay and Burt's study.
10. These were Baltimore, Chicago, Houston, and New York – cities with sizeable Korean immigrant population.
11. Readers interested in an analysis of the Korean children's utterance–internal language mixing (i.e. intra-sentential codeswitching) are referred to Shin (2002b).
12. Hakuta used Brown's (1973) scoring methods where the point of acquisition was defined as 'the first speech sample of three, such that in all three the morpheme is supplied in at least 90% of the contexts in which it is clearly required' (Hakuta, 1976: 334).
13. Dulay & Burt (1973) report that the order is virtually the same for both their Spanish- and Chinese-speaking subjects (Spearman rank order correlations of Spanish and Chinese groups: +0.95 ($p<0.001$)), an issue to which I return later in Chapter 5.

14. The total number of morphemes investigated varies. Brown originally listed 14 morphemes, of which Dulay and Burt investigated a subset of 11. Hakuta investigated 17, the current study 10 and Pak 12.

15. Note that the word 'watch' requires /IZ/ which is acquired slightly later than /s/ or /z/. However, the overall pattern of incorrect marking on nouns (except for the item 'sock') is also evident in 'watch'.

16. The two monolingual English-speaking children tested as controls in the current study marked all 24 of the plural nouns correctly, including the items 'sock' and 'shoe' with which most of their Korean peers had difficulty. This result is consistent with earlier studies of monolingual English-speaking children (e.g. Brown, 1973; De Villiers & De Villiers, 1985) which have reported that the plural -s is one of the earliest grammatical morphemes to be acquired by monolingual English-speaking children.

17. The small number of responses that have mixed Korean and English words (e.g. two **sinpal** [two shoes]) were assigned to either Column 'Correct K' or 'Incorrect K' depending on the word order.

18. For a detailed description of Korean grammar, see Martin (1992).

19. Over-reporting of church attendance/religiosity due to sampling bias is definitely likely however.

References

Andersen, R. (1978) An implicational model for second language research. *Language Learning* 28, 221–82.

Atkinson, J.M. and Heritage, J. (1984) *Structures of Social Action*. Cambridge: Cambridge University Press.

Auer, P. (1984) *Bilingual Conversation*. Amsterdam: Benjamins.

Auer, P. (1991) Bilingualism in/as social action: A sequential approach to code-switching. Paper read at the ESF Symposium on Code-Switching in Bilingual Studies: Theory, Significance and Perspectives, Barcelona, 21–23 March.

Auer, P. (1995) The pragmatics of code-switching: a sequential approach. In L. Milroy and P. Muysken (eds) *One Speaker, Two Languages: Cross-disciplinary Perspectives on Code-switching*. Cambridge: Cambridge University Press.

Auer, P. (ed.) (1998) *Code-switching in Conversation: Language, Interaction and Identity*. London: Routledge.

August, D. and Hakuta, K. (eds) (1997) *Improving Schooling for Language-Minority Children: A Research Agenda*. Washington, DC: National Academy Press.

Baker, C. (2000) *A Parents' and Teachers' Guide to Bilingualism* (2nd edn.). Clevedon: Multilingual Matters.

Baker, C. and Prys Jones, S. (1998) *Encyclopedia of Bilingualism and Bilingual Education*. Clevedon: Multilingual Matters.

Bailey, N., Madden, C. and Krashen, S. (1974) Is there a 'natural sequence' in adult second language learning? *Language Learning* 21(2), 235–243.

Bayley, R., Schecter, S.R. and Torres-Ayala, B. (1996) Strategies for bilingual maintenance: Case studies of Mexican-origin families in Texas. *Linguistics and Education* 8, 389-408.

Belluck, P. (1995) Healthy Korean economy draws immigrants home. The *New York Times*. 22 August, pp. A1, A12.

Bialystok, E. (2001) *Bilingualism in Development: Language, Literacy, & Cognition*. Cambridge: Cambridge University Press.

Bley-Vroman, R. (1990) The logical problem of second language learning. *Linguistic Analysis* 20, 3–49.

Boeschoten, H. (1990) Acquisition of Turkish by immigrant children: A multiple case study of Turkish children in the Netherlands aged 4 to 6. PhD thesis, Tilburg University.

Brown, R. (1973) *A First Language: The Early Stages*. Cambridge, MA: Harvard University Press.

Cancino, H., Rosansky, E.J. and Schumann, J.H. (1974) Testing hypotheses about second language acquisition: The copula and the negative in three subjects. *Working Papers in Bilingualism* 3, 80–96.

Cancino, H., Rosansky, E.J. and Schumann, J.H. (1975) The acquisition of the English auxiliary by native Spanish speakers. *TESOL Quarterly* 9, 421–430.

Carroll, S.E. (1998) On processability theory and second language acquisition. *Bilingualism: Language and Cognition* 1, 23–4.

Cazden, C.B. and Snow, C.E. (1990) *English Plus: Issues in Bilingual Education.* (The Annals of the American Academy of Political and Social Science). Newbury Park, CA: Sage.

Center for Applied Linguistics. (n.d.) Directory of two-way bilingual immersion programs in the USA. on www at http://cal.org/twi/directory/FMPro. Accessed 2 June 2003.

Chamot, A.U., Cummins, J., Kessler, C., O'Malley, M. and Wong Fillmore, L. (1996) *ScottForesman ESL: Accelerating English Language Learning.* Glenview, IL: Scott Foresman.

Cheshire, J. and Milroy, J. (1993) Syntactic variation in non-standard dialects: Background issues. In J. Milroy and L. Milroy (eds) *Real English* (pp. 3–33). London: Longman.

Cho, D. (2001) A wall of words: Many immigrants, children speak different languages. *The Washington Post,* 11 April, 2001, p. A01.

Cho, G. and Krashen, S. (1998) The negative consequences of heritage language loss and why we should care. In S.D. Krashen, L. Tse and J. McQuillan (eds) *Heritage Language Development* (pp. 31–39). Culver City, CA: Language Education Associates.

Cho, G. and Krashen, S. (2000) The role of voluntary factors in heritage language development: How speakers can develop the heritage language on their own. *ITL, Review of Applied Linguistics* 127–140.

Choe, Y.H. (1980) History. In H.K. Kim (ed.) *Studies on Korea: A Scholar's Guide* (pp. 27–47). Honolulu: University Press of Hawaii.

Chomsky, N. (1965) *Aspects of the Theory of Syntax.* Cambridge, MA: MIT Press.

Chong, K. (1998) What it means to be Christian: The role of religion in the construction of ethnic identity and boundary among second-generation Korean Americans. *Sociology of Religion* 59(3), 259–86.

Christian, D. and Genesee, F. (2001) *Bilingual Education. Case Studies in TESOL Practice Series.* Alexandria, VA: TESOL.

Clahsen, H. (1990) The comparative study of first and second language development. *Studies in Second Language Acquisition* 12, 135–53.

Clyne, M. (1984) The decade past, the decade to come: Some thoughts on language-contact research. *International Journal of the Sociology of Language* 45, 9–20.

Collier, V.P. (1987) Age and rate of acquisition of second language for academic purposes. *TESOL Quarterly* 21, 617–641.

Collier, V. (1992) A synthesis of studies examining long-term language-minority student data on academic achievement. *Bilingual Research Journal* 16 (1&2), 187–212.

Compton, C.J. (2001) Heritage language communities and schools: Challenges and recommendations. In J.K. Peyton, D.A. Ranard and S. McGinnis (eds) *Heritage Languages in America: Preserving a National Resource* (pp. 145–165). McHenry, IL: Center for Applied Linguistics and Delta Systems, Inc.

Corson, D. (2001) *Language Diversity and Education.* Mahwah, NJ: Erlbaum.

Couper-Kuhlen, E. and Selting, M. (eds) (1996) *Prosody in Conversation.* Cambridge: Cambridge University Press.

Crawford, J. (1992) *Hold Your Tongue: Bilingualism and the Politics of 'English Only.'* New York: Addison Wesley.

Crawford, J. (2000) How long to acquire a second language? *The Bilingual Family Newsletter* 17 (3), 4.

Crawford, J. (n.d.) *Guide to Title III of the No Child Left Behind Act*. On www at http://www.ourworld.compuserve.com/homepages/JWCRAWFORD/. Accessed 9 October 2002.

Crepin-Lanzarotto, P. (1997) Can you help me please? *The Bilingual Family Newsletter* 14(1), 1–2.

CrossCurrents. (1996) *Los Angeles Times* focuses on Korean American fascination for Harvard College. (Fall/Winter), 12.

Crystal, D. (1987) *The Cambridge Encyclopedia of Language*. Cambridge: Cambridge University Press.

Cummins, J. (1981) Age on arrival and immigrant second language learning in Canada: A reassessment. *Applied Linguistics* 2, 132–149.

Cummins, J. (1996) *Negotiating Identities: Education for Empowerment in a Diverse Society*. Ontario, CA: California Association for Bilingual Education.

Cummins, J. and Swain, M. (1986) *Bilingualism in Education: Aspects of Theory, Research and Practice*. London: Longman.

Dato, D.P. (1970) *American Children's Acquisition of Spanish Syntax in The Madrid Environment. Preliminary Edition*. US Office of Education. Institute of International Studies. Project No. 3036. Contract No. OEC 2-7-002637, May.

De Houwer, A. (1995) Bilingual language acquisition. In P. Fletcher and B. MacWhinney (eds) *The Handbook of Child Language*. Oxford: Blackwell.

De Klerk, V. (2000) Language shift in Grahamstown: A case study of selected Xhosa-speakers. *International Journal of the Sociology of Language* 146, 87–110.

De Mejia, A.-M. (1998) Bilingual storytelling: Code switching, discourse control, and learning opportunities. *TESOL Journal*, 7 (6, Winter), 4–10.

Demick, B. (2002) Lice to rice: Some in S. Korea opt for a trim when English trips the tongue. *Los Angeles Times*, 31 March.

De Villiers, J.G. and De Villiers, P.A. (1985) The acquisition of English. In D.I. Slobin (ed.) *The Crosslinguistic Study of Language Acquisition*. Hillsdale, NJ: Lawrence Erlbaum.

Döpke, S. (1997) Is the simultaneous acquisition of two languages in early childhood equal to acquiring each of the two languages individually? In E. Clark (ed.) *Child Language Research Forum 28* (pp. 95–112). Stanford, CA: Center for the Study of Language and Information.

Dulay, H.C. and Burt, M.K. (1973) Should we teach children syntax? *Language Learning* 23, 245–258.

Dulay, H.C. and Burt, M.K. (1974) Natural sequences in child second language acquisition. *Language Learning* 24(1), 37–53.

Ervin-Tripp, S. (1974) Is second language learning like the first? *TESOL Quarterly* 8, 111–127.

Fathman, A. (1975) Language background, age, and the order of English structures. Paper presented at the TESOL Convention, Los Angeles.

Felix, S.W. (1984) Maturational aspects of universal grammar. In A. Davies, C. Criper and A. Howatt (eds) *Interlanguage* (pp. 133–61). Edinburgh: Edinburgh University Press.

Feuerverger, G. (1989) Ethnolinguistic vitality of Italo-Canadian students in integrated and non-integrated heritage language programs in Toronto. *The Canadian Language Review* 46(1), 50–72.

Feuerverger, G. (1997) On the edges of the map: A study of heritage language teachers in Toronto. *Teaching and Teacher Education* 13, 39–54.

Fishman, J. (1976) *Bilingual Education: An International Sociological Perspective.* Rowley, MA: Newbury House.

Fishman, J.A. (1989) *Language and Ethnicity in Minority Sociolinguistic Perspective.* Clevedon: Multilingual Matters.

Fishman, J.A. (1991) *Reversing Language Shift.* Clevedon: Multilingual Matters.

Ford, C. and Thompson, S. (1996) Interactional units in conversation: Syntactic, intonational and pragmatic resources for the management of turns. In E. Ochs, E. Schegloff and S. Thompson (eds) *Interaction and Grammar* (pp. 134–84). Cambridge: Cambridge University Press.

Franklin, E. (1999) *Reading and Writing in More than One Language: Lessons for Teachers.* Alexandria, VA: TESOL.

Frauenfelder, U. (1974) The acquisition of French gender in Toronto French Immersion school children. Unpublished senior honors thesis, University of Washington.

Freeman, Y. and Freeman, D. (2000) An important strategy in multilingual classrooms. *NABE News* 24 (2), 20–21.

Gal, S. (1979) *Language Shift: Social Determinants of Linguistic Change in Bilingual Austria.* New York: Academic Press.

Gass, S.M. and Selinker, L. (2001) *Second Language Acquisition: An Introductory Course* (2nd edn). Mahwah, NJ: Erlbaum.

Genesee, F. (1989) Early bilingual language development: One language or two? *Journal of Child Language* 16, 161–179.

Giacalone Ramat, A. (1995) Code-switching in the context of dialect/standard language relations. In L. Milroy and P. Muysken (eds) *One Speaker, Two Languages: Cross-disciplinary Perspectives on Code-switching* (pp. 45–67). Cambridge: Cambridge University Press.

Goldberg, J. (1995) The overachievers. *New York* 28, (15, 10 April) 42–51.

Greek Orthodox Archdiocese of America (1999) *The Future of the Greek Language and Culture in the United States: Survival in the Diaspora.* New York, NY: Greek Orthodox Archdiocese of America.

Grimes, B.F. (ed.) (2000) *Ethnologue.* Dallas, TX: SIL International.

Grosjean, F. (1982) *Life with Two Languages.* Cambridge, MA: Harvard University Press.

Grosjean, F. (1985) The bilingual as a competent but specific speaker–hearer. *Journal of Multilingual and Multicultural Development* 6, 467–77.

Grosjean, F. (1989) Neurolinguists, beware! The bilingual is not two monolinguals in one person. *Brain and Language* 36, 3–15.

Gumperz, J.J. (1982) *Discourse Strategies.* Cambridge: Cambridge University Press.

Hakuta, K. (1976) A case study of a Japanese child learning English as a second language. *Language Learning* 26, 321–351.

Hakuta, K. (1987) The second-language learner in the context of the study of language acquisition. In P. Homel, M. Palij and D. Aaronson (eds) *Childhood Bilingualism: Aspects of Linguistic, Cognitive, and Social Development.* Hillsdale, NJ: Lawrence Erlbaum.

Hakuta, K. and Cancino, H. (1977) Trends in second language acquisition research. *Harvard Educational Review* 47, 294–316.

Hakuta, K. and D'Andrea, D. (1992) Some properties of bilingual maintenance and loss in Mexican background high-school students. *Applied Linguistics* 13, 72–99.

Hakuta, K. and Diaz, R.M. (1985) The relationship between degree of bilingualism and cognitive ability: A critical discussion and some new longitudinal data. In K.E. Nelson (ed.) *Children's Language* (Vol. V.). Hillsdale, NJ: Erlbaum.

Hakuta, K. and Mostafapour, E.F. (1996) Perspectives from the history and politics of bilingualism and bilingual education in the United States. In I. Parasnis (ed.) *Cultural and Language Diversity and the Deaf Experience* (pp. 38–50). New York: Cambridge University Press.

Hammersley, M. and Atkinson, P. (1995) *Ethnography: Principles in Practice*. (2nd edn.) London/New York: Routledge.

Harres, A. (1989) 'Being a good German': A case study analysis of language retention and loss among German migrants in North Queensland. *Journal of Multilingual and Multicultural Development* 10, 383–99.

Heath, S.B. (1983) *Ways with Words: Language, Life and Work in Communities and Classrooms*. Cambridge: Cambridge University Press.

Heller, M. (1982) Negotiations of language choice in Montreal. In J. Gumperz (ed.) *Language and Social Identity* (pp. 108–18). Cambridge and New York: Cambridge University Press.

Hinton, L. (1994) *Flutes of Fire: Essays on California Indian Languages*. Berkeley, CA: Heyday.

Hornberger, N.H. (1991) Extending enrichment bilingual education: Revisiting typologies and redirecting policy. In O. Garcia (ed.) *Bilingual Education. Focusschrift in Honor of Joshua A. Fishman* (pp. 215–34). Amsterdam and Philadelphia: John Benjamins.

Hornberger, N.H. (1998) Language policy, language education, language rights: Indigenous, immigrant, and international perspectives. *Language in Society* 27, 439–458.

Hurh, W.M. (1998) *The Korean Americans*. Westport, CT: Greenwood.

Hurh, W.M. and Kim, K.C. (1984) *Korean Immigrants in America: A Structural Analysis of Ethnic Confinement and Adhesive Adaptation*. Rutherford: Fairleigh Dickinson University Press.

Jefferson, G. (1972) Side sequences. In D. Sudnow (ed.) *Studies in Social Interaction* (pp. 75–110). New York: Free Press.

Jo, H.-Y. (2001) 'Heritage' language learning and ethnic identity: Korean Americans' struggle with language authorities. *Language, Culture and Curriculum* 14, 26–41.

Jo, M.H. (1999) *Korean Immigrants and the Challenge of Adjustment*. Westport, CT: Greenwood.

Kamwangamalu, N.M. (2003) Social change and language shift: South Africa. *Annual Review of Applied Linguistics* 23, 225–42.

Kelly, L.G. (ed.) (1969) *Description and Measurement of Bilingualism*. Toronto: University of Toronto Press.

Kim, B.L. (1977) Asian wives of US servicemen: Women in shadows. *Amerasia Journal* 5, 23–24.

Kim, B.L. (1978) *The Asian Americans: Changing Patterns, Changing Needs*. Montclair, NJ: Association for Korean Christian Scholars in North America.

Kim, B.L. (1988) The language situation of Korean Americans. In S.L. McKay and S.C. Wong (eds) *Language Diversity Problem or Resource? A Social and Educational Perspective on Language Minorities in the United States*. Boston, MA: Heinle and Heinle Publishers.

Kim, B.L., Sawdey, B. and Meihoefer, B. (1980) *The Korean-American Child at School and at Home: An Analysis of Interaction and Intervention through Groups.* Project Report (9-30-1978 through 6-30-1980). Project funded by administration for child, youth and families, US Department of Health, Education and Welfare, Grant 90-C-1335 (01).

Kim, E.H. and Yu, E.Y. (1996) *East to America: Korean American Life Stories.* New York: The New Press.

Kim, I. (1981) *New Urban Immigrants: The Korean Community in New York.* Princeton, NJ: Princeton University Press.

Kim, K.C. and Hurh, W.M. (1985) Ethnic resource utilization of Korean immigrant enterpreneurs in the Chicago minority area. *International Migration Review* 19, Spring.

Kim, K.C. and Hurh, W.M. (1993) Beyond assimilation and pluralism: Syncretic sociocultural adaptation of Korean immigrants in the US. *Ethnic and Racial Studies* 16(4), 696–713

Kim, S. (2003), Personal communication.

Kim, Y. (1997) The acquisition of Korean. In D.I. Slobin (ed.) *The Crosslinguistic Study of Language Acquisition* (Vol. 4.). Hillsdale, NJ: Lawrence Erlbaum.

Klein, W. (1986) *Second Language Acquisition.* Cambridge: Cambridge University Press.

Klesmer, H. (1994) Assessment and teacher perceptions of ESL student achievement. *English Quarterly* 26(3), 8–11.

Koehl, C. (1990) Minding the family store. *Newsweek* (special issue, winter 1989/spring 1990), 84.

Kondo, K. (1998) Social-psychological factors affecting language maintenance: Interviews with Shin Nisei University Students in Hawaii. *Linguistics and Education* 9, 369–408.

Köppe, R. and Meisel, J. (1995) Code-switching in bilingual first language acquisition. In L. Milroy and P. Muysken (eds) *One Speaker, Two Languages: Cross-disciplinary Perspectives on Code-switching.* Cambridge: Cambridge University Press.

Krashen, S. (1993) *The Power of Reading.* Engelwood, CO: Libraries Limited.

Krashen, S.D. (1998) Heritage language development: Some practical arguments. In S.D. Krashen, L. Tse and J. McQuillan (eds) *Heritage Language Development* (pp. 3–13). Culver City, CA: Language Education Associates.

Krashen, S.D., Tse, L. and McQuillan, J. (eds) (1998) *Heritage Language Development.* Culver City, CA: Language Education Associates.

Kulick, D. (1992) *Language Shift and Cultural Reproduction: Socialization, Self, and Syncretism in a Papua New Guinean Village.* Cambridge: Cambridge University Press.

Labov, W. (1972) *Language in the Inner City: Studies in the Black English Vernacular.* Philadelphia: University of Pennsylvania Press.

Lambert, W.E. (1955) Measurement of the linguistic dominance of bilinguals. *Journal of Abnormal and Social Psychology* 50, 197–200.

Lambert, W.E. (1977) The effects of bilingualism on the individual: Cognitive and socio-cultural consequences. In P. Hornby (ed.) *Bilingualism. Psychological, Social and Educational Implications* (pp. 15–28). New York: Academic Press.

Lanauze, M. and Snow, C. (1989) The relation between first- and second-language writing skills: Evidence from Puerto Rican elementary school children in bilingual programs. *Linguistics and Education* 1, 323–339.

Larsen-Freeman, D. (1975) The acquisition of grammatical morphemes by adult learners of English as a second language. PhD dissertation, University of Michigan.

Larsen-Freeman, D. and Long, M.H. (1991) *An Introduction to Second Language Acquisition Research.* London: Longman.

Lee, D.B. (1989) Marital adjustment between Korean women and American servicemen. *Korean Observer* 20, 321–352.

Lee, J.F.J. (1991) *Asian Americans: Oral Histories of First to Fourth Generation Americans from China, the Philippines, Japan, India, the Pacific Islands, Vietnam, and Cambodia.* New York: New Press.

Lee, J. (1995) Hankwuke swupwunlyusauy uymi pwunsek (A semantic analysis of Korean numeral classifiers). Masters thesis. Sangmyung University, Seoul.

Lee, J.S. (2002) The Korean language in America: The role of cultural identity in heritage language learning. *Language, Culture and Curriculum* 15 (2), 117-133.

Lee, K.O. (1997) Personal communication.

Leopold, W. (1939–49) *Speech Development of a Bilingual Child: Linguist's Record.* (Vols. 1–4.) Evanston, IL: Northwestern University Press.

Levinson, S. (1983) *Pragmatics.* Cambridge: Cambridge University Press.

Li, W. (1994) *Three Generations, Two Languages, One Family: Language Choice and Language Shift in a Chinese Community in Britain.* Clevedon: Multilingual Matters.

Li, W. (2000) Dimensions of bilingualism. In W. Li (ed.) *The Bilingualism Reader* (pp. 3–25). Routledge.

Li, W. (2002) 'What do you want me to say?': On the conversational analysis approach to bilingual interaction. *Language in Society* 31, 159–180.

Li, W. and Milroy, L. (1995) Conversational code-switching in a Chinese community in Britain: A sequential analysis. *Journal of Pragmatics* 23, 281–299.

Li, W.L. (1982) The language shift of Chinese-Americans. *International Journal of the Sociology of Language* 38, 109–124.

Lin, A.M.Y. (1988) Pedagogical and para-pedagogical levels of interaction in the classroom: A social interactional approach to the analysis of the codeswitching behavior of a bilingual teacher in an English language lesson. *Working Papers in Linguistics and Language Teaching* (University of Hong Kong Language Center), 11, 69–87.

Lin, A.M.Y. (1990) *Teaching in Two Tongues: Language Alternation in Foreign Language Classrooms.* (Research Report 3). Hong Kong: City Polytechnic of Hong Kong.

Lopez, M.E. (1999) *When Discourses Collide: An Ethnography of Migrant Children at Home and in School.* New York: Peter Lang.

Macedo, D. (2000) The colonialism of the English Only Movement. *Educational Researcher* 29 (3), 15–24.

Mackey, W.F. (1967) *Bilingualism as a World Problem/Le Bilinguïsme: Phénomène Mondial.* Montreal: Harvest House.

Macnamara, J. (1969) How can one measure the extent of one person's bilingual proficiency? In L.G. Kelly (ed.) *Description and Measurement of Bilingualism* (pp. 80–98). Toronto: University of Toronto Press.

Mangiafico, L. (1988) *Contemporary American Immigrants: Patterns of Filipino, Korean, and Chinese Settlement in the United States.* New York: Praeger.

Marcus, G. (1995) Children's overgeneralizations of English plurals: A quantitative analysis. *Journal of Child Language* 22, 447–59.

Marcus, G., Pinker, S., Ullman, M., Hollander, M., Rosen, T.J. and Xu, F. (1992) Overregularization in language acquisition. *Monographs of the Society for Research in Child Development* 57 (4, Serial No. 228).

Martin, S.E. (1966) Lexical evidence relating Korean to Japanese. *Language* 42, 185–251.

Martin, S.E. (1992) *A Reference Grammar of Korean: A Complete Guide to the Grammar and History of the Korean Language*. Rutland, VT: Charles E. Tuttle.

Martin-Jones, M. and Romaine, S. (1986) Semilingualism: A half-baked theory of communicative competence. *Applied Linguistics* 7(1), 26–38.

McClure, E.F. (1981) Formal and functional aspects of the code-switched discourse of bilingual children. In R.P. Duran (ed.) *Latino Language and Communicative Behavior* (pp. 69-94). Norwood, NJ: Ablex.

McLaughlin, B. (1978) The monitor model: Some methodological considerations. *Language Learning* 28, 309–332.

McQuillan, J. (1998) The use of self-selected and free voluntary reading in heritage language programs: A review of research. In S.D. Krashen, L.Tse and J. McQuillan (eds) *Heritage Language Development* (pp. 73–87). Culver City, CA: Language Education Associates.

Meisel, J. (1991) Principles of Universal Grammar and strategies of language use: On some similarities and differences between first and second language acquisition. In L. Eubank (ed.) *Point-Counterpoint: Universal Grammar in the Second Language* (pp. 231–76). Amsterdam: John Benjamins.

Milon, J. (1974) The development of negation in English by a second language learner. *TESOL Quarterly* 8, 137–143.

Milroy, L. and Gordon, M. (2003) *Sociolinguistics: Method and Interpretation*. Oxford: Blackwell.

Milroy, L. and Muysken, P. (eds) (1995) *One Speaker, Two Languages: Cross-disciplinary Perspectives on Code-switching*. Cambridge: Cambridge University Press.

Min, P.G. (ed.) (1995) *Asian Americans: Contemporary Trends and Issues*. Thousand Oaks, CA: Sage.

Min, P.G. (1996) *Caught in the Middle: Korean Merchants in America's Multi-ethnic Cities*. Berkeley, CA: University of California Press.

Moffatt, S. and Milroy, L. (1992) Panjabi/English language alternation in the classroom in the early school years. *Multilingua* 11 (4), 355–84.

Moon, I. (2001) A long trip to school: Why parents are enrolling kids abroad. *Business Week*, 27 August , 62–63.

Myers-Scotton, C. (1993) *Social Motivations for Codeswitching: Evidence from Africa*. Oxford: Clarendon Press.

National Association for Korean Schools. (2002) *The Korean American Journey*. New York: The National Association for Korean Schools.

National Center for Education Statistics (n.d.) Selected characteristics of public school teachers: Spring 1961 to spring 1996. On www at http://nces.ed.gov/pubs2002/digest2001/tables/dt070.asp Accessed 2 June 2003

Nicoladis, E. (1998) First clues to the existence of two input languages: Pragmatic and lexical differentiation in a bilingual child. *Bilingualism: Language and Cognition* 1, 105–116.

Ochs, E. and Schieffelin, B. (1995) The impact of language socialization on grammatical development. In P. Fletcher and B. MacWhinney (eds) *The Handbook of*

Child Language (pp. 73–94). Cambridge, MA: Blackwell.

O'Grady, W. (1991) *Categories and Case: The Sentence Structure of Korean*. Amsterdam: John Benjamins.

Pak, Y. (1987) Age differences in morpheme acquisition among Korean ESL learners: Acquisition order and acquisition rate. PhD Dissertation, University of Texas, Austin.

Paradis, J. and Genesee, F. (1996) Syntactic acquisition in bilingual children: Autonomous or interdependent? *Studies in Second Language Acquisition* 18, 1–25.

Park, K. (1997) *The Korean American Dream: Immigrants and Small Business in New York City*. Ithaca, NY: Cornell University Press.

Pearson, B.Z., Fernandez, S. and Oller, D.K. (1995) Cross-language synonyms in the lexicons of bilingual infants: One language or two? *Journal of Child Language* 22, 345–368.

Perlstein, L. (2000) Few Asian Americans attracted to teaching: School systems competing for a limited supply. *The Washington Post*, 1 February, B1.

Pfaff, C.W. (1992) The issue of grammaticalization in early German second language. *Studies in Second Language Acquisition* 14, 273–296.

Pfaff, C.W. (1993) Turkish language development in Germany. In G. Extra and L. Verhoeven (eds) *Immigrant Languages in Europe* (pp. 119–146). Clevedon: Multilingual Matters.

Pfaff, C.W. (1994) Early bilingual development of Turkish children in Berlin. In G. Extra and L. Verhoeven (eds) *The Cross-linguistic Study of Bilingual Development* (pp. 75–97). Amsterdam: Netherlands Academy of Arts and Sciences.

Poplack, S. (1980) Sometimes I'll start a sentence in English y termino en espanol: Toward a typology of code-switching. *Linguistics* 18, 581–618.

Portes, A. and Hao, L. (1998) E Pluribus Unum: Bilingualism and loss of language in the second generation. *Sociology of Education* 71, 269–294.

Pucci, S. (1994) Supporting Spanish language literacy: Latino children and free reading resources in the schools. *Bilingual Research Journal* 18, 67–82.

Putz, M. (1991) Language maintenance and language shift in the speech behavior of German-Australian migrants in Canberra. *Journal of Multilingual and Multicultural Development* 12, 477–92.

Quay, S. (1995) The bilingual lexicon: Implications for studies of language choice. *Journal of Child Language* 22, 369–87.

Ramirez, J.D. (1992) Executive summary. *Bilingual Research Journal* 16(1/2), 1–62.

Ravem, R. (1968) Language acquisition in a second language environment. *International Review of Applied Linguistics in Language Teaching* 6, 175–185.

Ravem, R. (1974) The development of Wh-questions in first and second language learners. In J.C. Richards (ed.) *Error Analysis: Perspectives on Second Language Acquisition*. London: Longman.

Redlinger, W. and Park, T. (1980) Language mixing in young bilinguals. *Journal of Child Language* 7, 337–52.

Richards, B. and Yamada-Yamamoto, A. (1998) The linguistic experience of Japanese preschool children and their families in the UK. *Journal of Multilingual and Multicultural Development* 19, 142–157.

Romaine, S. (1983) Collecting and interpreting self-reported data on the language use of linguistic minorities by means of 'language diaries'. *MALS Journal* 9, 1–30.

Romaine, S. (1995) *Bilingualism*. Oxford: Blackwell.

Ronjat, J. (1913) *Le Développement du Langage Observé chez un Enfant Bilingue.* Paris: Champion.

Scarcella, R. and Chin, K. (1993) Literacy Practices in Two Korean-American Communities. (National Center for Research on Cultural Diversity and Second Language Learning Research Report 8.) Santa Cruz, CA: National Clearing House for English Language Acquistions and Language Instruction Educational Programs.

Schachter, J. (1998) The need for converging evidence. *Bilingualism: Language and Cognition* 1, 34–5.

Schecter, S.R. and Bayley, R. (1997) Language socialization practices and cultural identity: Case studies of Mexican-descent families in California and Texas. *TESOL Quarterly* 31, 513–541.

Schegloff, E. (1998) Reflections on studying prosody in talk-in-interaction. *Language and Speech* 41, 235–63.

Schieffelin, B.B. (1994) Code-switching and language socialization: Some probable relationships. In J.F. Duchan, L.E. Hewitt and R.M. Sonnenmeier (eds) *Pragmatics: From Theory to Practice.* Englewood Cliffs, NJ: Prentice Hall.

Schwartz, A.M. (2001) Preparing teachers to work with heritage language learners. In J.K. Peyton, D.A. Ranard and S. McGinnis (eds) *Heritage Languages in America: Preserving a National Resource* (pp. 229–252). McHenry, IL: Center for Applied Linguistics and Delta Systems, Inc.

Schwartz, B.D. and Sprouse, R.A. (1994) Word order and nominative case in nonnative language acquisition: A longitudinal study of (L1 Turkish) German Interlanguage. In T. Hoekstra and B.D. Schwartz (eds) *Language Acquisition Studies in Generative Grammar* (pp. 317–68). Amsterdam: John Benjamins.

Scotton, C.M. (1976) Strategies of neutrality: Language choice in uncertain situations. *Language* 52, 919–41.

Scotton, C.M. (1980) Explaining linguistic choices as identity negotiations. In H. Giles, W.P. Robinson and P.M. Smith (eds) *Language: Social Psychological Perspectives* (pp. 359–66). Oxford: Pergamon.

Scotton, C.M. (1982) The possibility of code-switching: Motivation for maintaining multilingualism. *Anthropological Linguistics* 24, 432–43.

Scotton, C.M. (1983) The negotiation of identities in conversation: A theory of markedness and code choice. *International Journal of the Sociology of Language* 44, 115–36.

Shannon, S.M. (1999) The debate on bilingual education in the US: Language ideology as reflected in the practice of bilingual teachers. In J. Blommaert (ed.) *Language Ideological Debates* (pp. 171–199). Berlin: Mouton de Gruyter.

Shin, S.J. (2002a) Birth order and the language experience of bilingual children. *TESOL Quarterly* 36(1), 103–113.

Shin, S.J. (2002b) Differentiating language contact phenomena: Evidence from Korean–English bilingual children. *Applied Psycholinguistics* 23, 337–60.

Shin, S.J. and Milroy, L. (1999) Bilingual language acquisition by Korean schoolchildren in New York City. *Bilingualism: Language and Cognition* 2, 147–67.

Shin, S.J. and Milroy, L. (2000) Conversational codeswitching among Korean–English bilingual children. *International Journal of Bilingualism* 4, 351–83.

Skutnabb-Kangas, T. (1984a) *Bilingualism or Not: The Education of Minorities.* Clevedon, England: Multilingual Matters.

Skutnabb-Kangas, T. (1984b) Children of guest workers and immigrants: Linguistic and educational issues. In J. Edwards (ed.) *Linguistic Minorities, Policies and Pluralism* (pp. 17–48). London: Academic.

Skutnabb-Kangas, T. (2000) *Linguistic Genocide in Education: Or Worldwide Diversity and Human Rights?* Mahwah, NJ: Erlbaum.

Slobin, D.I. (ed.) (1985/1992) *The Crosslinguistic Study of Language Acquisition* (3 Vols). Hillsdale, NJ: Lawrence Erlbaum.

Slobin, D.I. (1988) The development of clause chaining in Turkish child language. In S. Koç (ed.) *Studies in Turkish Linguistics.* Ankara: Middle East Technical University.

Slobin, D.I. (ed.) (1997) *The Crosslinguistic Study of Language Acquisition* (Vol. 4) Hillsdale, NJ: Lawrence Erlbaum.

Snow, C.E. (1990) Rationales for native language instruction: Evidence from research. In A.M. Padilla, H.H. Fairchild and C.M. Valadez (eds) *Bilingual Education: Issues and Strategies* (pp. 60–74). Newbury Park, CA: Sage.

Snow, C.E. and Hakuta, K. (1992) The costs of monolingualism. In J. Crawford (ed.) *Language Loyalties: A Source Book on the Official English Controversy* (pp. 384–94). Chicago: University of Chicago Press.

Sohn, S.-O. (n.d.) *Korean language development and academic achievement of Korean Americans in the Los Angeles Unified School District.* On www at http://www.humnet.ucla.edu/flr/heritage/papers/sohn.htm Accessed on 11 October 2002.

Sridhar, K.K. (1988) Language maintenance and language shift among Asian-Indians: Kannadigas in the New York area. *International Journal of the Sociology of Language* 69, 73–87.

Swain, M. and Cummins, J. (1979) Bilingualism, cognitive functioning and education. *Language Teaching and Linguistics: Abstracts* 12, 4–18.

Swain, M. and Lapkin, S. (1982) *Evaluating Bilingual Education: A Canadian Case Study.* Clevedon: Multilingual Matters.

Taft, R. and Cahill, D. (1989) Mother tongue maintenance in Lebanese immigrant families in Australia. *Journal of Multilingual and Multicultural Development* 10, 129–43.

Thomas, W.P. and Collier, V.P. (2002) *A National Study of School Effectiveness for Language Minority Students' Long-term Academic Achievement.* Santa Cruz, CA: Center for Research on Education, Diversity and Excellence.

Timm, L. (1975) Spanish–English code-switching: el Porque y how not to. *Romance Philology* 28, 473–482.

Tse, L. (1996) Language brokering in linguistic minority communities: The case of Chinese- and Vietnamese-American Students. *Bilingual Research Journal* 20, 485–98.

Tse, L. (1998a) Ethnic identity formation and its implications for heritage language development. In S.D. Krashen, L. Tse and J. McQuillan (eds) *Heritage Language Development* (pp. 15–29). Culver City, CA: Language Education Associates.

Tse. L. (1998b) Affecting affect: The impact of heritage language programs on student attitudes. In S.D. Krashen, L. Tse and J. McQuillan (eds) *Heritage Language Development* (pp. 51–72). Culver City, CA: Language Education Associates.

Tse, L. (2001) Resisting and reversing language shift: Heritage-language resilience among US native biliterates. *Harvard Educational Review* 71, 676–708.

Tucker, G.R. (1991) Developing a language competent American society: The role of language planning. In A.G. Reynolds (ed.) *Bilingualism, Multiculturalism, and Second Language Learning*. Hillsdale, NJ: Lawrence Erlbaum.

Tuominen, A. (1999) Who decides the home language?: A look at multilingual families. *International Journal of the Sociology of Language* 140, 59–76.

Unterbeck, B. (1994) Korean classifiers. In Y.K. Kim-Renaud (ed.) *Theoretical Issues in Korean Linguistics*. Stanford: CSLI Publications.

Vainikka, A. and Young-Scholten, M. (1994) Direct access to X'-theory: Evidence from Korean and Turkish adults learning German. In T. Hoekstra and B.D. Schwartz (eds) *Language Acquisition Studies in Generative Grammar* (pp. 265–316). Amsterdam: John Benjamins.

Valadez, C.M., MacSwan, J. and Martinez, C. (2000) Toward a new view of low-achieving bilinguals: A study of linguistic competence in designated 'semilinguals.' *Bilingual Review* 25(3), 238–248.

Valdés, G. (1996) *Con Respeto: Bridging the Distances Between Culturally Diverse Families and Schools*. New York: Teachers College Press.

Valdés, G. (2003) *Expanding Definitions of Giftedness: The Case of Young Interpreters from Immigrant Communities*. Mahwah, NJ: Lawrence Erlbaum Associates.

Verhoeven, L. (1988) Acquisition of discourse cohesion in Turkish. In S. Koç (ed.) *Studies in Turkish Linguistics*. Ankara: Middle East Technical University.

Verhoeven, L.T. and Boeschoten, H.E. (1986) First language acquisition in a second language environment. *Applied Psycholinguistics* 7, 241–56.

Verhoeven, L.T. and Vermeer, A. (1985) Ethnic group differences in children's oral proficiency of Dutch. In G. Extra and T. Vallen (eds) *Ethnic Minorities and Dutch as a Second Language* (pp. 105–32). Dordrecht, Holland: Foris Publications.

Vihman, M. (1985) Language differentiation by the bilingual infant. *Journal of Child Language* 12, 297–324.

Volterra, V. and Taeschner, R. (1978) The acquisition and development of language by bilingual children. *Journal of Child Language* 5, 311–26.

Wells, B. and MacFarlane, S. (1998) Prosody as an interactional resource: Turn-projection and overlap. *Language and Speech* 41, 265–94.

White, L. (1989) *Universal Grammar and Second Language Acquisition*. Amsterdam: John Benjamins.

Wiley, T.G. (2001) On defining heritage languages and their speakers. In J.K. Peyton, D.A. Ranard and S. McGinnis (eds) *Heritage Languages in America: Preserving a National Resource* (pp. 29-36). McHenry, IL: Delta Systems and Center for Applied Linguistics.

Willig, A.C. (1985) A meta-analysis of selected studies on the effectiveness of bilingual education. *Review of Educational Research* 55, 269–317.

Wode, H. (1976) Developmental sequences in naturalistic L2 acquisition. *Working Papers on Bilingualism* 11, 1–31.

Wode, H. (1978) Developmental principles in naturalistic L2 acquisition. In E. Hatch (ed.) *Second Language Acquisition: A Book of Readings*. Rowley, MA: Newbury House Press.

Wong Fillmore, L. (1991) When learning a second language means losing the first. *Early Childhood Research Quarterly* 6, 323–346.

Wong Fillmore, L. (2003) External pressures on families. In R. Campbell and D. Christian (eds) *Directions in Research: Intergenerational Transmission of Heritage Languages*. Heritage Language Journal 1 (1), 9–12.

World Alamanac. (2003) *The World Almanac and Book of Facts 2003*. New York: World

Almanac.

Young, R. and Tran, M. (1999) Language maintenance and shift among Vietnamese in America. *International Journal of the Sociology of Language* 140, 77–82.

Zentella, A.C. (1997) *Growing Up Bilingual: Puerto Rican Children in New York.* Malden, MA: Blackwell.

Zobl, H. and Liceras, J. (1994) Functional categories and acquisition orders. *Language Learning* 44 (1), 159–180.

Appendix 1: List of Abbreviations

ACC	Accusative
CLASS	Classifier
COP	Copula
DAT	Dative
DECL	Declarative
DEL	Delimiter
FUT	Future tense
HON	Honorific
NOM	Nominative
PAST	Past tense
PRES	Present tense
TOP	Topic marker

Appendix 2: Transcription Conventions

The transcription of conversational data in this book adapts procedures in Conversation Analysis as used by Atkinson and Heritage (1984). The following are the most frequent conventions used:

(.)   A micropause less than a second duration.
(*n*)   A timed pause where *n* is the duration of the pause in seconds.
:   A long vowel.
::   A longer vowel.
/   Indicates utterance boundary.
!   Indicates an animated tone, not necessarily an exclamation.
?   Indicates a rising intonation, not necessarily a question.
=   Links contiguous utterances (adjacent utterances with no interval in between).
[Overlapping utterances.
[

Appendix 3: The Yale system of romanization

Hangul	Yale	Basic phonemic realization	Hangul	Yale	Basic phonemic realization
ㅂ	p	/p/	ㅔ	ey	/e/
ㅍ	ph	/ph/	ㅖ	yey	/ye/
ㅃ	pp	/p'/	ㅞ	wey	/we/
ㄷ	t	/t/	ㅚ	oy	/æ/
ㅌ	th	/th/	ㅐ	ay	/e/ , /æ/
ㄸ	tt	/t'/	ㅒ	yay	/ye/ , /yæ/
ㅅ	s	/s/	ㅙ	way	/we/ , /wæ/
ㅆ	ss	/s'/	ㅡ	u	/w/
ㅈ	c	/č/	ㅓ	e	/ə/
ㅊ	ch	/čh/	ㅕ	ye	/yə/
ㅉ	cc	/č'/	ㅝ	we	/wə/
ㄱ	k	/k/	ㅏ	s	/a/
ㅋ	kh	/kh/	ㅑ	ya	/ya/
ㄲ	kk	/k'/	ㅘ	wa	/wa/
ㅁ	m	/m/	ㅜ	wu	/u/
ㄴ	n	/n/	ㅠ	yu	/yu/
ㅇ	ng	/o/	ㅗ	o	/o/
ㄹ	l	/l/	ㅛ	yo	/yo/
ㅎ	h	/h/	ㅟ	uy	/ui/
ㅣ	i	/i/			
ㅟ	wi	/wi/			

Source: O'Grady (1981).

Appendix 4. Questionnaire for Parents

1. Sex: (circle one)   Male   Female

2. Age: _____

3. Place of birth: _____

4. How long have you lived in the United States? _____ years

5. What is the highest academic degree you have? (Circle one)
    a. elementary school   b. middle school   c. high school   d. college
    e. graduate school

6. Circle the appropriate answer.
    a. How well do you understand Korean?
        Not at all   not well   fairly well   very well
    b. How well do you speak Korean?
        Not at all   not well   fairly well   very well
    c. How well can you read in Korean?
        Not at all   not well   fairly well   very well
    d. How well can you write in Korean?
        Not at all   not well   fairly well   very well
    e. How well do you understand English?
        Not at all   not well   fairly well   very well
    f. How well do you speak English?
        Not at all   not well   fairly well   very well
    g. How well can you read in English?
        Not at all   not well   fairly well   very well

h.   How well can you write in English?
        Not at all   not well   fairly well   very well

7.   What other languages do you know? _____

8.   State each of your children's sex and age.
        First-born child: Male ___, Female ___; Age _____
        Secondborn child: Male ___, Female ___; Age _____
        Thirdborn child: Male ___, Female ___; Age _____

9.   Do you send your children to weekend Korean school? (Circle one) Yes
        No
        Why or why not?

_____

10.   (Circle one for each) What language do you normally use at home
        when discussing personal and domestic matters
        a)   with spouse?   Korean   English   Korean and English
        b)   with children? Korean   English   Korean and English
        c)   with parents?   Korean   English   Korean and English

11.   (Circle one for each) What language do you normally use when
        discussing current happenings in Korea
        a)   with spouse?   Korean   English   Korean and English
        b)   with children? Korean   English   Korean and English
        c)   with parents?   Korean   English   Korean and English

12.   (Circle one for each) What language do you normally use when
        discussing current happenings in the States
        a)   with spouse?   Korean   English   Korean and English
        b)   with children? Korean   English   Korean and English
        c)   with parents?   Korean   English   Korean and English

13.   (Circle one for each child) What language do you normally use in
        speaking to
        a)   your First-born child?   Korean   English   Korean and English
        b)   your Second-born child? Korean   English   Korean and English
        c)   your Third-born child?   Korean   English   Korean and English

14. Which of your children do you speak the most Korean with?
    a) First-born child
    b) Second-born child
    c) Third-born child

15. Which of your children do you speak the most English with?
    a) First-born child
    b) Second-born child
    c) Third-born child

16. Do you remember what age each of your children started speaking English?
    a) First-born child: _____ years old
    b) Second-born child: _____ years old
    ca) Third-born child: _____ years old

17. What language did each of your children use in speaking to you before entering school? (Circle one for each child)
    a) your First-born child: Korean   English   Korean and English
    b) your Second-born child: Korean   English   Korean and English
    c) your Third-born child: Korean   English   Korean and English

18. What language did each of your children use in speaking to you after entering school? (Circle one for each child)
    a) your First-born child: Korean English Korean and English
    b) your Secondborn child: Korean English Korean   and English
    c) your Thirdborn child: Korean English Korean and English

19. Which of your children talks with the mother the most?
    a) First-born child
    b) Secondborn child
    c) Thirdborn child

20. Which of your children talks with the father the most?
    a) First-born child
    b) Secondborn child
    c) Thirdborn child

21. Which of your children has the highest proficiency in Korean? (Circle one)
    a) First-born child
    b) Secondborn child
    c) Thirdborn child

22. Which of your children has the highest proficiency in English? (Circle one)
    a) First-born child
    b   Secondborn child
    c) Thirdborn child

23. Which of your children likes to speak Korean the most? (Circle one)
    a) First-born child
    b) Secondborn child
    c) Thirdborn child

24. Which of your children likes to speak English the most? (Circle one)
    a) First-born child
    b) Secondborn child
    c) Thirdborn child

25. Do you belong to any church? (Circle one)   Yes _____   No _____
    If yes, what language do you normally use in speaking to other church members? (Circle one) Korean   English   Korean and English

26. Who takes care of the children in the family?_____

27. What language does the children's caretaker normally use in speaking to the children?
    Korean   English   Korean and English   Other _____

28. When any of your children is playing alone, what language does he/she use in speaking to himself/herself? (Circle one for each child)
    a) your First-born child: Korean   English   Korean and English
    b) your Secondborn child   Korean   English   Korean and English
    c) your Thirdborn child: Korean   English   Korean and English

29. When your children ask you for something (e.g. a new toy/money etc.) what language do they normally use? (Circle one for each child)
    a) your First-born child: Korean   English   Korean and English
    b) your Secondborn child: Korean   English   Korean and English
    c) your Thirdborn child: Korean   English   Korean and English

30. When you discuss with your children their schoolwork, what language do you normally use?_____

31. If your children speak to you in English and you reply in Korean, what language would your children continue the conversation in? (Circle one for each child)
    A) your First-born child: Korean   English   Korean and English
    B) your Secondborn child: Korean   English   Korean and English
    c) your Thirdborn child: Korean   English   Korean and English

32. If your children speak to you in English and you don't understand, what do you usually do? _____

33. If your children speak to you in English and you don't understand, what do they usually do? _____

34. How do you feel about your children speaking English to each other at home? _____

35. How do you feel about your children using mixed Korean and English in speaking to you? _____

36. How do you feel about your children speaking English to you in the presence of your Korean friends/relatives?

_____

37. Do you teach your children Korean? (Circle one)   Yes   No

38. Do you read to your children in Korean? (Circle one)   Yes   No

39. Do you teach your children English? (Circle one)   Yes   No

40. Do you read to your children in English? (Circle one)   Yes   No

41. What language do you feel more comfortable speaking at home? (Circle one)
     English   Korean   either mixed English and Korean

42. What language do you feel more comfortable speaking outside home? (Circle one)
     English   Korean   either   mixed English and Korean

43. What language do you prefer your children speak to you at home? (Circle one)
     English   Korean   either   mixed English and Korean

44. What language do you prefer your children speak to you outside home? (Circle one)
     English   Korean   either   mixed English and Korean

45. What reasons would you give to your children for learning English?

     _____

46. What reasons would you give to your children for learning Korean?

     _____

47. If your children had the chance to study one of the several foreign languages in their schools, what would you ask them to choose? (circle one)
     Spanish French German Korean Chinese Japanese Italian
     Other _____

48. Do you wish to send your children to Korea to learn Korean? (Circle one)   Yes   No

49. Would you be interested in seeing a heritage Korean language class offered at your children's schools? (circle one)   Yes   No

50. How do you feel about a Korean living in the States not being able to speak Korean?

    _____

51. How do you feel about a Korean living in the States not being able to speak English?

    _____

52. Do you have difficulties in bringing up your children in the States? (circle one)
    Yes   No
    If yes, what are they? _____

53. What do you consider yourself? (circle one)
    Korean   American   equally Korean and American

Author Index

Subject Index